The Language of the
BLACK EXPERIENCE

For Naty

The Language of the BLACK EXPERIENCE

*Cultural Expression through Word and Sound
in the Caribbean and Black Britain*

Edited by
DAVID SUTCLIFFE
and
ANSEL WONG

Basil Blackwell

© Basil Blackwell Ltd 1986

First published 1986

Basil Blackwell Ltd
108 Cowley Road, Oxford OX4 1JF, UK

Basil Blackwell Inc.
432 Park Avenue South, Suite 1503,
New York, NY 10016, USA

British Library Cataloguing in Publication Data

The Language of the black experience: cultural
expression through word and sound in the
Caribbean and black Britain.
1. English language——Social aspects——Great
Britain   2. Blacks——Great Britain——Language
I. Sutcliffe, David   II. Wong, Ansel
306'.4   PE1073
ISBN 0-631-13425-5
ISBN 0-631-14816-7 Pbk

Library of Congress Cataloging in Publication Data
The Language of the Black experience.

Includes bibliographies and index.
1. Blacks——Caribbean Area——Languages——
Addresses, essays, lectures.   2. Blacks——Great
Britain——Languages——Addresses, essays,
lectures.   3. Sociolinguistics——Caribbean Area——
Addresses, essays, lectures.   4. Sociolinguistics——
Great Britain——Addresses, essays, lectures.
I. Sutcliffe, David, M. Ed.   II. Wong, Ansel.
P40.5.B42L3 1986   401'.9'08960729   85-20129
ISBN 0-631-13425-5
ISBN 0-631-14816-7 (pbk.)

Typeset by Katerprint Typesetting Services Ltd, Oxford
Printed in Great Britain

Contents

Murder! Disya one mean ME!
My name is Sister B
From de black community.
Me come fe tell you
Bout me per-son-a-li-ty.

A fragment of 'rappin' or 'toastin' from a black newspaper in Britain

Acknowledgements

Our thanks go to all the people who made this book possible: the contributors, James Berry especially for his encouragement, the Caribbean Community of Dudley and the New Testament Church of God, and the Caribbean Community of Watford and the Church of God in Christ. We would also like to thank Mª Antonia Heredero and Patricia Leguía for typing parts of the manuscript, Joanne Neffe for her helpful comments and suggestions and Natividad Pablos for her great support. And, finally, we also would like to thank Mr Mistry and Mrs Althea Gooden of Watford Community Relations organization for their help.

For permission to reprint copyright material the editors and publishers would like to acknowledge the following with gratitude:

Arista Records Inc. and Almo Publications for 'If she don't want your lovin'' 1982, Irving Music Inc. and Lwesrika Music (BMI), all rights reserved, int'l copyright secured (p. 26); Leosongs Copyright Bureau for the excerpted Bob Marley song published by Cayman Music Inc. administered by Leosong Copyright Service Ltd, 4A Newman Passage, London W1. (p. 116); Mr Hopton Edwards for the excerpted Bunny Wailer song (p. 115); Allison & Busby for the material from George Lamming's *The Emigrants* (p. 80); Anvil Press for the excerpt from E. A. Markham's 'Inheritance' (p. 83); Black Ink Collective for the excerpt from Jawiattika Blacksheep's 'Discrimination' (p.87); Centerprise Trust Ltd for the excerpt from Vivian Usherwood's 'My Name is I don't know' (p. 92); Alfred A. Knopf Inc. and Laurence Pollinger Ltd for material from V. S. Reid's *New Day* (pp. 71–2); *Limestone* magazine for the excerpt from E. A. Markham's 'Love at No. 13' (p. 98); Thomas Nelson and Sons Ltd for material from Geoffrey Drayton's 'Christopher' (pp. 73–4); Race Today Publications for the excerpts from Linton Kwesi Johnson's 'Want Fi Goh Rave' (p. 84) and 'It Dread Inna Inglan' (p. 90); and all the writers and performers whose works are excerpted in chapters 5 and 6.

D. S.
A. W.

Notes on Contributors

DAVID SUTCLIFFE was born in England in 1943 and taught in secondary schools before his interest in black language and culture led him to take up full-time writing and research in 1978. He is the author of *British Black English* (1982).

CAROL TOMLIN was born in Yorkshire. She has taught in secondary schools and carried out fieldwork for linguistic research – both in the West Midlands. She is at present teaching in Oxford for the Multi-Cultural Advisory Centre and studying for a master's degree at Birmingham University. She is a Pentecostal Christian.

The Rev. L. A. JACKSON was born in Jamaica in 1938. He emigrated to Britain in 1959 and became a British citizen. He is a member of the New Testament Church of God, of which he is an ordained minister, and he has recently gained a degree in Bible theology. He spends his spare time writing poetry.

JAH BONES was born in Kingston, Jamaica, in 1940, was called to the Rastafari faith in 1957 and came to Britain in 1962. He has a bachelor's degree in social sciences and is an organizer, writer, editor and activist.

JAMES BERRY was born in Jamaica and came to Britain in 1948. A poet, commentator and lecturer, active in both schools and writers' workshops, his publications include: *Bluefoot Traveller* (1976), *Fractured Circles* (1979), *Lucy's Letters and Loving* (1982) and *News for Babylon* (1984).

ANSEL WONG was born in Trinidad but completed his education in Britain. He has taught in secondary schools in London and was formerly head of AHFIWE School, an off-site centre for truants, disruptives and under-achievers. He was, until April 1986, Principal Race Relations Adviser to the Greater London Council.

JOHN RICHMOND was born in 1951. He worked for the Inner London Education Authority from 1974 to 1985, first in two comprehensive schools and then as an Advisory Teacher for English. He is currently Project Officer for the School Curriculum Development Committee's National Writing Project.

PETRONELLA BREINBURG was born in multi-cultural, multi-lingual Surinam (formerly Dutch Guyana). She has been a teacher and lecturer in South America, Britain, the Netherlands, Belgium and Germany. She has also published books for children and short stories and has written plays for theatre-in-education. She is at present a post-doctoral research fellow attached to the Linguistics Department of the University of Sheffield.

MARK SEBBA was born in 1956. He trained as a theoretical linguist and was awarded a doctorate by the University of York in 1984. Between 1981 and 1984 he worked on a research project related to the sociolinguistics of London Jamaican.

MORGAN DALPHINIS was born in St Lucia and came to Britain at the age of 11. His doctorate, from the School of Oriental and African Studies, University of London, was on African influences in Creole languages. He is at present Senior Lecturer in Multi-Ethnic Education at Hackney College, London. He has published a number of poems in Creole and English.

Introduction

DAVID SUTCLIFFE

Society

Caribbean migrants came to Britain in the two decades following the Second World War, seeking employment and educational opportunity for their children and bringing with them a dimension to what is now called a multi-cultural British society. The new dimension was and still is poorly understood by the white majority. This is hardly surprising – superficial similarities between the cultures mask some fundamental differences, and superficial contact between the communities in schools and at work mask a basic lack of communication between Caribbean and white British. The control of education, television, radio and the press is overwhelmingly in the hands of whites, so blacks find it hard to take stock, to obtain a representative picture of what they are and what they are about.

James Berry once wrote of Caribbean people in Britain that they are grossly under-explored, under-expressed and under-contributing. Despite this, at the level of day-to-day interaction in the milieux of church, club and blues dances and in writing for pleasure or specialized publication there has been no lack of self-expression – quite the reverse. The sense of identity has been sharpened by the climate of indifference and non-publication described by Berry, and this is the theme of this book. The essays within it explore ways in which the community is expressing its world view, its selfhood, through its own developed verbal power and word music. There is plainly a need to provide a faithful reflection of this expression, understood within the context of African and Caribbean history and present experience. In doing so it is important to strike a balance between viewing this oral culture in Britain as an irritant, as protest and reaction, and viewing it as existing in its own right as creativity, a celebration of a certain world view and aesthetics. Both are true, but the latter in a sense encompasses the former, and in the context of being part of an ethnic minority the use of such aesthetics is in itself a declaration, almost a protest. The contributors to this book explore this expression within the contemporary British setting, but inevitably they deal also with the earlier stages, the African and Caribbean roots and the comparatively recent developments on both sides of the Atlantic, and with the process of continuance and alteration, of shift of emphasis. None of the writers' contributions deals with phenomena that have no antecedents, with new counter-cultures that are just British – except, arguably, Chapter 9, on London Jamaican. The latter language could be said to have both black and white antecedents that it blends into a new form and yet manages to retain as separable strands.

I use 'black' to mean culturally black almost more than biologically black. And the same is true of Afro-Caribbean. Jamaica has a mixture of peoples but basically one roots culture, strongly Caribbean – and, I would argue, more Afro-Caribbean than anything else. I shall continue to use 'black' in this way to refer to a culture and identity that is rooted in the Caribbean and in Africa, that continues to grow and to absorb other influences into its original cultural matrix. The term must be understood in this context.

Despite the prevailing climate of misunderstanding and misinformation that I have described, there is a growing interest in black culture at several levels of mainstream British society, not only at the level of academic research or among teachers but also, perhaps most sincerely and frankly, among some young white people in the cities who are adopting black idiom and intonation. The impact that these features are having on the English language as they ripple out through the wider society has been described as the greatest since Caxton. Young whites – and, indeed, Asians too – can now be heard describing themselves as looking 'well hard', referring to someone in an embarrassing situation as 'shamed up' and using 'Guy!' as an exclamation, complete with a black inflection of the voice. The attraction is the aesthetics and the vigour of the language and the realization that in the present context it symbolizes a defiant declaration against oppressive forces.

It would be good to think that all this signals the beginning of the fulfilment of George Lamming's distant dream. Lamming concluded in one of his essays (in *Pleasures of Exile*, 1960) that black people and white, whom he saw prefigured in Shakespeare's Caliban and Prospero, must work together in the context of a new horizon so that the psychological legacy of their original contract will be annulled. Clearly we have a long way to go, and clearly the desirable goal of the destruction of the bitter bond of racism does not spell integration. Black people now want, and always will want, cultural freedom. At present, however, the need for blacks to create this cultural space for themselves is urgently and insistently evoked by the climate of racism. This necessity remains a constant behind all the varieties of lifestyle and degrees of blackness and whiteness that young blacks may exhibit.

Language

Language has been described as that which makes us uniquely human, uniting us all. It also divides us. It refracts the light of experience through many different systems of expression and embodies it in many different oral traditions. It is both highly stable, reflecting the linguistic systems of previous generations, and capable of tremendous flexibility, including innovation in vocabulary, idiom, pronunciation and even grammar. This stability is due partly to the social situation in which language is learned and developed, in the family and in wider social networks, although it also has to do with the systematic nature of language itself. Black language in Britain today exhibits this creative stability and variation to a remarkable degree, above all in the tension between Jamaican Creole and English.

Caribbean Creoles had their origin in the late seventeenth and early eighteenth centuries, scarcely more than twelve generations ago, when black people from many different parts of West and Central Africa were thrown together on the Caribbean plantations. They created their own new social networks: white people were not only generally excluded but also actively opposed through them. With the forging of these new affiliations across the old tribal divisions, new common languages had to be created. The origin of the grammatical systems of these languages is a question for academic debate. Some scholars see them as fusions of African grammars and others as manifestations of a universal grammar common to all human beings, on which the Africans had to draw. Morgan Dalphinis sees strong evidence for African input – I agree. What is indisputable is that the early Afro-Americans drew heavily on the colonial language – English, French or whatever it might have been – for their vocabulary. They had limited access to this, in a seventeenth- or eighteenth-century and probably regional form and, of course, interpreted it through their African patterns of reception and production of speech. And very plainly too these new-created language systems, with their (largely) European-derived words pronounced in a distinctively African way, were the medium for the Africans' own culture and oral traditions, in large part a continuation of the ancestral traditions. To give an example from the present day, when a British black person quotes the Creole proverb 'Fala-fashn mongki brok ím nek' (Follow-fashion monkey bruck him neck), every word is from English. The pronunciation is different, and above all the intonation is different, showing a family resemblance to the tonal systems of certain African languages. The grammar differs from English in having a verb form /brok or *bruck*/ that remains invariant whether used for the simple present or simple past, and *im* shows its possessive role, as meaning 'his' (im nek). /Falla-fashn/ is a characteristically Caribbean kind of compound meaning 'copycat' or 'blind follower'. Finally, the situation in which the proverb might be used is typically Afro-American: it may be quoted by an older person advising or correcting a younger; equally it may be used in verbal duelling as a 'put-down' remark.

In appreciating how this new Afro-American culture was created in the Caribbean it is important to realize that behind the enormous number of different African language groups involved – each, for instance, with its own name for God and its own pantheon of lesser gods – there was a common core of African culture from which a synthesis could be made. There is no doubt that black people from widely separated parts of the Americas share a common bond of blackness that is more than skin-deep. Take as an example the case of a concert in England in which the performers may be black American, the audience drawn from different parts of the Caribbean (as well as young people born in Britain). All participate as black people and very clearly show common norms of behaviour in terms of participation in the performance and response to the music, both in what they respond to and how they respond. We can argue over how much of this is due to the common African inheritance and how much to the common past of the Middle Passage and the plantations – how much the pearl is due to the oyster and how much to the intruding grit.

In Afro-American culture(s) the world of oral language as experience, as performance, is dominantly important. In the beginning was the word, and for many black people the word, or more comprehensively the voice, provides the expression of what the Rastafarians call 'powah', the life-energy used by black people creatively whether in concert, church sermon, debate or street-corner conversation. It was this tradition of orality, and the proverbial lore associated with it, that post-war Caribbean migrants brought to Britain, the oral culture so well documented, for instance, in Michael Thelwell's novel *The Harder They Come*. What has happened to that culture since then shows the stability and adaptation, the continuity and change, we have already touched on. They came, like Ivan/Rhygin in Thelwell's book, to an unfamiliar urban situation where they had to adapt their social mores and change some basic conclusions about life but could not slough off the premises of their culture. Like Ivan/Rhygin, theirs was a journey to disillusionment, not this time in Kingston but in the 'Motherland' itself. Because of the idealistic picture of British life and values that they had imbibed through their education, they expected to be welcome, and at home, in their new country, a country that was in some way going to be familiar territory. They were unprepared for the scarcely disguised hostility they met when they sought housing or employment – unprepared but not totally amazed, since in Britain they finally confronted the reality that they had always tried not to contemplate, the squalidly racist view which many white people have inherited of blacks, as a legacy from slavery and colonialism. They were genteelly shunned by some, called 'wogs' by others, but the accumulated negative message of the centuries was the same – and what liberals thought in their upper-middle-class retreats was more or less irrelevant.

In dealing with this, a jarring psychological shock for most, however they eventually fared, they had to draw on reserves of strength within themselves, and collectively as a people. In this there is something of a paradox. Black people have through their history developed a resilience to shocks of this kind and a collective feeling of their ability to deal with life. Yet this same history carries the message that the white person is an eternal problem yet holds out salvation, economic and educational – or, rather, makes the rules by which this salvation can be obtained. They say a cockroach never gets justice when the fowl judges. This, the negative side of the Caribbean cultural inheritance, is what Rastafarians seek to overcome with their new-wrought language, where, for instance, what they see as the slave *mi* of Jamaican Creole is replaced in their speech by the active pronoun I (or, better still, I-an-I), representing the individual united with God and his fellows.

Many of the people have derived strength and solace from the black Churches, which have provided them with a social space in which *they* make the rules, in which *they* can develop and succeed. The Churches have afforded them spiritual strength derived in a typically black way – from collective, joyful worship in which the love of God is experienced – and continue to be a very important and underrated force.

The first generation of settlers also looked to their children for the success they themselves had never enjoyed. They hoped that their children, Caribbean- or British-born, would profit from a British education and would gain the qualifications that ought to give access to the higher-paid occupations previously denied to blacks, apparently because of their lack of schooling. Of course, some black migrants themselves had good qualifications, and perhaps these people had few illusions about how difficult the path to career success was going to be.

Harking back to Lamming's dream, we could say that one obvious forum where black and white might work together to form a new vision of themselves and their relationship is education. Education has the potential to change according to the needs of its clients and is a key area. However, as an institution it tends to guard jealously its own conservatism, its own right to control knowledge and access to success in the job market.

It is now well known that on the whole black children have not been doing well in British education. It has been established that they often meet with prejudice when they leave school and look for employment. From the start (in the 1960s, in fact) black children and their parents tended to feel misunderstood by the teachers (Sutcliffe, 1978), even in primary schools where all children were 'just children' and overt racism among staff was rare. In the secondary school, with many black children destined for the lower streams on intake, the situation was more acute. These days the racism of the wider society has drained many black children of motivation. They see the uphill task of doing well in the education system as being rewarded with a lower-paid job – or no job at all, given the present level of unemployment – allotted by a society that does not wish them well or at best wishes them to gain the least valuable prizes, fill the lowest strata in the labour market. The cynicism that then sets in, perhaps allied to the positive aim of enjoying school at the expense of the teacher, is documented in *The Black Explosion in British Schools* (Dhondy, 1982). Of course, not all black children and not all schools fail, or fail as badly as described here. But almost all black pupils feel that school, although less racist than the wider society, has in some way given them short change – for example, in not providing a positive image of black people in the curriculum and in underrating black people in general.

With this raising of awareness of racism, particularly during mid-adolescence, the secondary-school period, there comes a raising of black consciousness: an awareness that black people can express their identity through their own language, music and lifestyles and can find solutions to their problems within the community. One of the clearest markers of this process is the growing use of the British form of Creole, or 'Patois' as it is usually called by people who speak it. Significantly, in most areas of Britain this is of Jamaican derivation even when the speakers' parents are from other parts of the Caribbean. One way of explaining this is to point to the greater number of settlers from that island – some 60 per cent of the total Caribbean migration – and to the influence of reggae and Rastafarianism. Equally significant is the fact that young people of disparate Caribbean family origins feel a common bond and so come together, for instance, in their use of language. Teachers tend to notice this use of Patois among pupils in early or mid-adolescence and then view it as an effort to build a new counter-culture when

in fact, as Jah Bones discusses in Chapters 3 and 4, it is a
renewal, a culture that is a counter to white encroachment
(rather than a counter-culture) and is made to last well
beyond adolescence. And younger black children can also
speak a form of Creole, though more circumspectly. What
might be called 'open' use of Patois can be seen as a form of
protest, but its symbolic role has a number of dimensions.
Ansel Wong discusses these, while in the penultimate chapter
Mark Sebba gives a linguist's description of the language
itself. There is a parallel between the way in which young
Afro-Caribbean people in Britain decide to use Creole
'openly' and the role of that language in the Caribbean when
used very overtly, unexpectedly. 'Breaking away into Creole',
proclaiming 'dramatic low status', letting 'one's lips run
away' with one, 'going on ignorant', or 'making a heaven of a
noise': these are various ways of describing it. Creole has in
England a 'fiesty' (rude, impudent) role shading through to a
serious 'roots' role. We may note too, in connection with
what was said earlier about black language as protest and
nuisance or as self-justifying and admirable, that key cultural
terms symbolize this. *Bad* or *wicked*, for instance, can have
the normal pejorative meaning *or* the meaning 'morally bad'
(but admirable) *or* the meaning 'admirable' in terms of black
aesthetics. *Dread*, because of its serious roots connection, has
only the first (as in the novelist Wilson Harris's concept) or
the third meaning (as in Rasta).

Patois gives access to, and identity with, a rich complex of
cultural activity, from street level up. Without this blacks in
Britain would be in a vacuum, culturally deprived in that they
would have a set of Caribbean tastes and norms in music,
lyrics and language left unsatisfied. And activity on both sides
of the Atlantic is linked by black language and culture. The
link with Jamaica – 'JA', 'Jam down', 'Jah-mek-ya' or plain
'Backayard' – is especially strong despite all the particularity
of the black scene in Britain, the forging of a new, shifting,
changing urban slang and so on (see Marcia Smith in Sutcliffe, 1982).

Many of the points made in this introduction are negative.

The problem for black youth – young men and women – lies very much in their relations with the mainstream white community: policing, education, schooling and employment. The frustrations of having white employers and teachers controlling one's life chances, and above all white police controlling and invigilating and defining one as potentially criminal, build waves of tension that may issue in harmless verbal confrontations or may, on rare but unforgettable occasions, erupt into a Brixton 1981 or a Handsworth or Tottenham 1985. The percentage of blacks involved in these disturbances is very small, but everyone inside in the community understands why they occur, whether he or she condones them or not. Faced with these problems on a day-to-day basis, black people want to recreate their own lives and culture, on various levels and as they see fit. Rasta is just one of the most vivid examples, involving a Copernican reorientation of the self. Just as central is the recognition that the grammar, structure and style of the cultural world described in this book are important, subjectively and objectively, and that to sell these for a mess of Anglo-Saxon potage is a sterile act.

It should also be recognized that two factors or institutions are taking out the heat, the destructive energy, at present as in the past. They are the black Churches and Rasta. Obviously, Rastas do not conform with 'Babylon' in the way that black Christians do in many outward respects. But Rastas have a moral code, talk of righteousness. They believe in dialogue (reasoning). They take up an 'I'm OK, you're OK' position as soon as the dialogue establishes that this is possible – a common tendency among black people as a whole. Marxists argue that black youth is revolutionary. It is, but more in the sense described by Bones and Berry than in the purely political-materialist sense. There is no question that Marxism is the tool for analysing the political-social structure confronting young blacks. Marxism is less successful, I would argue, in analysing their response (though see Wong's chapter on power and solidarity). Christians, in fact, succeed in the system but in some (genuine) respect are not *of* the system.

Perhaps we should say that they succeed parallel to the system – they have, for instance, recently opened a national college of their own at Overton.

In the chapters of this book many positive factors emerge. Prejudice does not easily diminish, but, as Berry once remarked to me in a letter, people have a way of coming right, of being guided by their subconscious. Berry has a poet's perceptions, not a sociologist's, but writers are aware of the power of such subconscious connections. The influential white Columbian novelist Gabriel Garcia Marquez has said, 'The Caribbean taught me to see reality in a different way ...' Garcia Marquez (1982) was stunned to find, when he visited Angola for the first time, that culturally he was part-African, that the special Caribbean consciousness he 'learnt' as a child and developed as a novelist had come from Africa. Such learning and insights lift us above racism.

Within black circles in Britain there is a feeling of creativity, particularly in music and language. There is what Berry calls the 'culture-spirit' and Jah Bones (taking a more African stance) describes as the 'African spirit, emotion and instinct of an African people' (quoted from 'Words of Wisdom', *Caribbean Times*). This spirit repeats itself throughout the culture, through the medium of sound and its structuring into music and language. This culture spirit *is* African in its root origin. It has dialogued with the many ethnic groups that came after to the Caribbean and to continental America. It has dialogued, and continues to do so, with the 'West', with Babylon, and gains access or channels of communication through the international media of music and English.

There are very deep implications, ultimately: on one level opportunities for studying cultural continuity and change, on another the development of a particular kind of aesthetics and world view that strangely parallels modern physics in its waves, particles, vibrations and interactive forces. The time is ripe for such study. James Snead, in a recent essay (1984), argues convincingly, 'The outstanding fact of late twentieth-century European culture is its ongoing reconciliation with black culture'. Perhaps most important, there are implications for human relationships, for looking at them (and living them) in terms of what we could call an I-an-I model of expanded consciousness. Something of the kind is necessary, I believe, if we are to survive into the twenty-first century. Black culture suggests, and Rasta implicitly shows, that it will be done best through dialogue.

Part One

The Cultural Experience

1

The Black Churches

DAVID SUTCLIFFE AND CAROL TOMLIN

The black Pentecostal Churches in Britain, unlike Rasta, have attracted almost no scholarly attention. Perhaps this is because they are not a purely adolescent phenomenon and have a predominantly female membership. But the black churches are, in terms of organization, resources and numbers, the single most important institution in the black community. For this reason alone their language would be of interest, especially as a growing proportion of their congregations comes from the British-born generation. In fact, the Churches are theatres of language performance. And in their language, aesthetics and spirituality they show a clear debt to Africa. The music too – increasingly black American in style these days – is often very 'roots' and, at its best, superb.

Pentecostalism in Jamaica dates from the earliest decades of this century. Its introduction and expansion immediately predate the first stirrings of Rastafarianism. The impetus for the establishment of Pentecostalism came from America, and indeed many of the black Pentecostal Churches in Britain have their headquarters in the United States. The Church of God in Christ is one example; the New Testament Church of God is another. There were aspects of these Churches that immediately suited them for uptake by the Jamaican population. First, their ideology: they preached the influx of the Holy Spirit as an experience open to believers, as in the first Pentecost when the Disciples were gathered in an upper room

(Acts 2). This notion – and experience – holds particular significance for those with an African or an Afro-American world view, as we shall see. Secondly, their services, as a collective act of worship or as an individual quest for this influx of the Spirit, used very distinctively black forms of interaction, of communication and celebration of the Christian message. Thus the religiousness of Afro-Americans in the Caribbean (and in the United States, where Pentecostalism was founded) has been reinterpreted as Pentecostal Christianity. Despite its teachings based on careful reading of the Bible and its approach to God through Jesus it now fits into an Afro-Caribbean cultural matrix extraordinarily well.

The Move to Britain

It has been estimated that some 70 per cent of the migrants who came to Britain in the 1950s and early 1960s were regular church-goers. In the main the churches attended were Pentecostal (a substantial minority of migrants were Seventh Day Adventists). Those who were not regular church-goers would have had ties of family or friendship with those who were and shared broadly the same background, folk belief and so on.

There is no room here to document in any detail the experience of black people arriving in Britain and expecting to find a new road to personal fulfilment but finding themselves instead in a cul-de-sac closed in by rejection and hostility. Like the Middle Passage of two or three hundred years ago, it is an experience that has etched itself into the collective memory of the people whose language and culture form the theme of this book. Apart from their dismal difficulties in finding accommodation and employment, black migrants were dismayed to learn that Britain, the 'Motherland', was a country where the majority were not practising Christians. There were further difficulties when they attended local churches on the first occasions. First – and here we are generalizing from anecdotal evidence drawn from this generation – they tended to feel snubbed by their white fellow

Christians: perhaps not overtly confronted by racial hostility but vaguely excluded. There are stories of sandwiches being handed round after the service and of their not being offered to new black members and so on. The other difficulty lay in the style of worship, which in the great majority of Roman Catholic, Anglican and Nonconformist churches would have seemed cold, uncommunicative, emotionally inexpressive. Even in Salvation Army gatherings and other 'joyful' types of services extensive cultural and doctrinal differences would have checked the Caribbean worshippers in their search for spiritual experience. They were all Christians, black and white, yet short of purging themselves of their Afro-Caribbean background, blacks had no choice but to continue to find Christ in their own way or cease to be practising Christians. Many took this latter option, it seems.

After these difficulties, and the gradual absorption of some of the mores of life in Britain, a diminished number were determined to continue with their Christianity and sought to set up their own Churches. Through their common bond of race, culture and experience they were intent on remaining spiritually intact. And numbers subsequently grew steadily.

The pattern was for a congregation to gather round a particular pastor, meeting at first in homes and in any halls which were available, forming links with other black congregations and with Jamaican/American headquarters. The congregations soon acquired church premises that had fallen into disuse with the increasing secularization of British society and the drift away from inner-city areas. In some cases they raised money to put up new church buildings – an indication of the organized impetus of this section of the black community, of its ability to draw upon its own resources. From these beginnings the Churches flourished. In 1964 there were twenty-three congregations belonging to the New Testament Church, for instance, the largest of the black Pentecostal Churches in Britain. Today it has some eighty-eight congregations with a regular membership of over 8,000.

These Churches are very active and make substantial demands on their members. There are usually two Sunday services, each generally lasting between two and four hours (if no outside restriction is imposed on their duration). There are also Sunday school classes, further services during the week and choir rehearsals – nearly all churches have their choirs, which now frequently consist of younger, usually British-born, members. Additionally, there are many special events during the year, including area or 'district' conventions and 'building programmes' (services held expressly to raise money). There are also concerts, sometimes attracting literally thousands of black Christians to different venues to enjoy the singing of choirs, groups and individuals. Very often nowadays this singing veers towards the black American style (gospel music), and the virtuosity displayed is stunningly impressive.

It is plain that over the years the social and spiritual life of these Churches has acted as a buffer against the negative forces of discrimination, the demoralizing effects of being part of a black minority in a white racist society. In this the black Churches compare and contrast with Rastafarianism, since the latter also offers spiritual solace but with a different doctrinal rational. Black Christians discover their worth in experiencing God (Christ), which unites them not only with God but also with their fellow Christians. They approach this experience as black people (Afro-Caribbeans) without normally describing this process as African in any way.

Rastas find God (Jah) within themselves, which integrates them psychologically and socially with fellow believers. They consciously look to Africa not only as their cultural heritage but also as their future, and they overtly express the value of blackness/Africanness. Black Christians live in the world of white society but not of it. Rastas live in a street world (largely black) but not of it. Both groups have a 'moral' code. Both groups are, typically, more racially isolated than black non-believers in terms of their social contacts. Black Christians spend a large proportion of their non-working time either at church or socializing with church members (congregations on average, at a conservative estimate, are 99 per cent black – that is, of African or part-African descent). Rastas, who again are overwhelmingly (but not exclusively) black, spend most of their time either with other Rastas or at least in locales where most or all of the people available to socialize with are also black.

Black Churches continue to attract younger members and obtain a firm commitment from them. A high percentage of these are female. Here there is an inverse relationship with Rastafarianism, in that the majoirty of Rastas are male, though their preponderance is not so extreme. Males within a Church are likely to consist of the pastor (invariably male) and perhaps one or two young aspiring pastors, men over the age of 40 (still outnumbered by females of their age), young musicians who accompany the services on drums, guitars and a keyboard instrument, and very few others.

Speech Events in Black Worship

Writing of the black Churches in the United States, similar in many ways to black Churches in the Caribbean and Britain, Geneva Smitherman (1981: 90) has it that they 'may be defined as that in which the content and religious substance has been borrowed from the Western Judaeo-Christian tradition, but the communication of that content – the process – has remained essentially African'. This makes the act of worship itself essentially African, yet Christian, since the process of communication is all-important in black oral culture generally – in a sense the medium is the message (the religious experience in this case).

To focus on the verbal interaction in black church services, let us look at three speech events within this context – preaching, testimony and prayer – and relate these events to the Afro-American oral tradition and its ethnography of speaking.

The main preaching event in the service is the sermon, usually delivered by the pastor, though sometimes by other members of the congregation. Black preachers are usually endowed with 'the gift of the gab' and are verbally very flexible. Although many preachers prepare their sermons, in that they study the Bible, they depend on divine guidance to lead them and do not keep strictly to a prepared lecture. This approach is in keeping with the Pentecostal belief in the power of the Spirit and allows preachers to respond to, and work with, the congregation.

The constant in this unrehearsed improvisation is their ability to preach in a black preaching style. To answer the question 'What makes this preaching style different?' we have to examine the verbal devices and verbal forms that create a style peculiar, to a great extent, to black preachers.

The black preaching language can be characterized in a number of ways. In addition to the spontaneity and improvisation already mentioned, there are call-and-response, proverbial expression, exaggerated language, image-making and metaphor, and tonal sound effects.

Call-and-response refers to the very pervasive black cultural trait whereby an audience either echoes or adds to the utterances of the performer. In black church sermons preacher/congregation rapport and support is established and built up in this way. The congregation is not just a passive audience but an active body of participants, who interject such responses as 'Amen', 'Preach it, preacher', 'Yes', 'Hmh-hmh', 'Come on now, preacher.' Many preachers call on the audience for the desired response and may say, for instance, 'Come on, church.' If touching on a sensitive spot a preacher may say, 'I don't get no amen' or 'You gone quiet on me, church.'

As mentioned earlier, sermons are not rigorously planned, since the turn and direction of a particular message should depend upon the 'leading of the Holy Spirit'. With this spontaneity at his disposal the preacher is free to detect the mood of the audience and to respond to this verbally or non-verbally. Improvisation is evident, for example, in the way many preachers highlight the points they are making by means of digressions. These serve to bring the sermon to life, to make it relevant to the experience of the congregation.

Similarly, proverbial expressions, which are common not just to black churchgoers but to black people as a whole, are used in sermons to enlighten, elaborate and drive points home with force. They may say: 'Wha sweet nanny goat wi run him belly' ('What a nanny goat craves will upset her stomach'), referring to temptation and sin and their unfortunate results; or 'Spit in the sky and it fall ina you face' ('Every action brings a reaction').

Proverbs and proverbial expression, incidentally, have their roots in the African cultural linguistic pattern and have been retained by West Indians. The image-making of black preaching style is closely related. Concrete imagery and fable both shade into proverbs and proverbial expressions. A preacher likens the Christian life to a journey on the motorway. A pastor compares the true Christian not with the hen who gives her eggs but with the pig who, in giving, gives its all. A young British-born woman, in a devotional sermon, says that the aspiring Christian travels a road with detours, wrong turnings, road works and missed signs but with true determination to reach the end of the journey, come what may. She builds the images one by one, to end amid tremendous applause.

Black preaching style is also dependent on what Geneva Smitherman calls 'tonal semantics' (Smitherman 1981, p. 99). In this, verbal power can be achieved through the use of words and phrases carefully chosen for their sound and their mediation through what is virtually an African tonal system. Usually this is in conjunction with language that has a poetic or flowery nature: 'The church is a place not of entertainment but amazement', 'Man's extremities are God's opportunity', 'The source of the force is the Holy Ghost.' This last, in Jamaican Creole is: dí súòs á dí fúòs á dí húòlí gúòs.* The /úò/ sounds and the overall tonal pattern dramatically reinforce the message.

In addition to these verbal devices there are non-verbal communicative devices that also mark black preaching style. The black preacher is usually very agile; he uses not only his hands and his feet but his entire body to communicate. A

* The diacritics that indicate high tone (') and low tone (') are based on the work of Carter and Sutcliffe (1982).

particular body stance may convey a special meaning. One preacher, for instance, after making a very important point, makes short, stomping foot movements. Another preacher places his leg on the railing of a rostrum to illustrate how the rich will be judged by God. We find the dynamics of call-and-response not only between preacher and congregation but in practically every aspect of the service – in testimonies, for instance, and in individual prayer, when group response is evident. Testimonies are offered by members and tell of God's goodness, divine visitation and spiritual experience. Testimonies have to be regarded as very important because of the fundamental view among black Pentecostalists that one should express one's spiritual experience. Consequently, members are encouraged not to be afraid but to 'stand up and testify'. Indeed, the exteriorizing of one's thoughts and feelings, having a viewpoint and expressing it, is part of Afro-American culture generally (see, for instance, Kochman, 1981). One finds even very young members of Churches testifying and thus adopting the verbal strategies of the old.

In testimonies the verbal art of the Caribbean is superbly displayed. One can hear highly poetic language, expressive language, symbolic speech, a singing-talking tonal effect and group interaction. In testimonies one can also hear the shift, particularly among the older members, from English to Creole, especially when the person who is testifying becomes more intense and emotionally involved. Thus Creole is often the medium of expression for the deep-seated feelings of the heart.

Testimonies have a particular format. Usually the person who testifies begins with: 'Shall we praise the Lord?' (Congregational response: 'Praise the Lord.') This formula may be repeated several times, occasionally becoming an event in itself, building to a high level of emotional or spiritual intensity. Often the testifier quotes from a verse of a song or from the Bible and thus he or she creates and sets the scene:

Amazing grace, how sweet the sound
That saved a wretch like me.
I once was lost, but now I'm found,
Was blind but now I see.

The testifier usually relates the particular verse to his or her spiritual experience. Expression is frequently poetic/symbolic, combining biblical imagery with West Indian dramatic delivery: 'The Psalmist David said: "Oh, taste and see that the Lord is good. Blessed is the man that trusteth in him. I thank the Lord for that blessed night when he called me out of the miry fields of sin, and I have tasted of that great salvation" ' (Sister Walters, Dudley).

Since music forms such an integral part of Caribbean culture, it is interesting to note that a musical quality is detectable in much Caribbean speech, especially in marked emotional, dramatic or ritual declarations. Testimonies frequently become literally lyrical, especially on the lips of older members: 'I'm thanking God for saving my soul. I'm thanking God for making me whole. Tonight I'm feasting in a wonderful and free salvation. I'm asking you to pray for me whilst I do the same for you. I mean to continue in Jesus' name' (Sister Smith, Dudley).

A rhyming or poetic effect is frequently evident. Since testimonies often begin with a verse of a song, the talking-rhyming effect emerges, and this frequently adds to the repertoire of popular formulae:

I'm thanking God for saving my soul.
I'm thanking God for making me whole.
I'm thanking God for giving me
The blessed victory.
When I was lost in sin,
Jesus came and took me in.

(Brother Simpson, Dudley)

Group interaction comes into play in the testimonies. Murmurs and shouts of 'Amen', 'Praise the Lord' are uttered at certain intervals, and these serve to encourage the person who is testifying to verbalize his or her thoughts. And when a testimony is concluded the congregation always says, 'Praise the Lord.'

This support and rapport is also an important element in prayer. Prayer can be divided into two main categories: congregational and individual. Congregational prayer is collective prayer, which involves all in praying aloud at the same time. Individual prayer occurs when an individual prays aloud while the rest of the congregation listens and supports, or sometimes two or three individuals may pray simultaneously or alternately.

To listen to the individual prayer of black Pentecostals is a moving experience. In praying the power of speech becomes a potent force. Prayer is highly revered. Not only is prayer seen as a spiritual connection but it is viewed as a spiritual gift – there are those who, it is believed, are spiritually endowed with the verbal gift of prayer. Such individuals are often called upon to pray with articulate and powerful expression, and they invariably do so. Prayer is always extemporary. There is neither set text nor preparation. It is fascinating to note that, when composing 'on their feet', individuals in prayer do not stop to ponder or search for words but maintain a rhythm, a flow of language. Deriving from the rich verbal and cultural heritage of the Caribbean, this articulate volubility in prayer is given enabling support by the congregation. Audience rapport is of paramount importance. Verbal responses such as 'Hallelujah', 'Yes, Lord', 'Thank you, Jesus' can be heard during prayer. The dynamics of such speech events involve the communication of both participant and responder: the participant relies upon the response of the congregation for the cue for the duration of the prayer, and as the shouts of 'Amen' become intensified, the person who is praying is borne up on to a high plateau of spiritual ecstasy. Black Pentecostals are assured of divine scriptural guidance on the matter of how to pray, for the New Testament talks of the Spirit being able to express our innermost thoughts. This tallies with their belief in the power of the Holy Spirit.

The particularities of the ethnography of speaking in black

Pentecostal services are found in secular contexts of black culture(s) with an insistence, regularity and geographic spread that serve only to underline emphatically what we have already stated, that there is a fostering of black cultural traits, essentially Africanisms, within black worship. First there is the call-and-response pattern (group rapport and support) noted in preaching, in testimonies and in prayer and found throughout church services. This is amen-saying, the 'Right on' of black Americans and the 'scene/seen' of young black people in Britain. Attentiveness in the Afro-American world is usually shown by sympathetic vocalization and movement, not by silent, immobile listening. As we have already mentioned, the pattern of call-and-response is evident in its most exaggerated form in black church services when a testifier or moderator leads a series of repetitions of 'We praise the Lord.' The congregation echoes each repetition of this phrase, sometimes reaching a crescendo of feeling.

Call-and-response is a pattern of communication that occurs throughout the Afro-American world. For example, the Saramaccans of the Surinam forests, with a culture that is probably Afro-American in its purest form, show a very clear-cut pattern of call-and-response in their storytelling. Every line of the story uttered by the narrator is greeted by a response from the listener: 'Yes', 'That it is so', 'Indeed.'

In black American storytelling in the United States the response of the listener may be less formalized but is otherwise comparable. Joel Chandler Harris describes a particular instance of this process in his introduction to *Nights with Uncle Remus*. When he was waiting for his train one night in Georgia 1882 he sat with a group of black railroad workers and, 'by way of a feeler', told the Tar Baby story. As he told the tale, 'The comments of [one] worker ... were loud and frequent. "Dar now!" he would exclaim, or "He's a honey, mon!" or "Genterman's git out de way an' gin 'im room" ' (Hemenway, 1982).

Associated with this call-and-response pattern is the tendency for speakers sometimes to overlap their utterances with those of others – not in a totally ungoverned way, although the overall impact may seem chaotic or overwhelming to a

European. Frequently one or two lead speakers, with support from others, will voice their variations on the theme in a way that causes partial or complete overlap. (For a description of such resonant, 'multi-track' conversations in Antigua, see Reisman, 1974.)

Call, response and overlap have featured in black music since the earliest days of slavery. In modern gospel, soul and funk music both are very frequent. A good example is the song 'If she don't want your lovin'' by the black American artist Aretha Franklin, in which the backing group and lead singer respond to and overlap each other, together building the performance:

ARETHA: (*Singing*) Let me take { you off her hands
CHORUS: { Let me take you off her hands
ARETHA: and show you what you can do { with a real woman
CHORUS: { show you what a real
ARETHA: baby . . .
CHORUS: woman . . .
ARETHA: (*talking*) come here, boy. Let me { show you what you can
CHORUS: { She don't want
ARETHA: do with a real woman
CHORUS: She don't want . . .
ARETHA: Yeah, give it to me – I'll take it.
          (*singing*) Let me take . . . { you off
CHORUS: Let me { take . . . you off her hands.
ARETHA: Show you what you can do . . .
CHORUS: Show you what you can do
ARETHA: . . . with a real
CHORUS: with a real woman

Sound, Motion and the Spirit

The spiritual ecstasy of black churches is striking, almost tangible, destined to leave an indelible impression on the visitor. Its effect springs from several causes. There is the ethnography of speaking, the process of communication which we have already described; there is the overall intensity of the sound and motion, and the spiritual intensity associated with this. Inextricably linked with these is the mystical experience, the touching of members of the congregation by the Holy Ghost.

A central element of the primal religions of Africa is the experience of being filled with the power of the spiritual. The material world is seen to be invested with forces that may be directed by human agencies, living or dead, or may be purely by spiritual agencies. These forces provide the ultimate causality for all events. Worshippers expect to be able to enter this underlying world of the spirit by seeking to be possessed by an ancestor or deity. Similarly, black Pentecostals exercise and release deep emotional feelings as a reaction to the power of the Holy Spirit.

This is the culminating experience for the worshippers, not always achieved. As it appears in black Pentecostal worship it is culturally related to the Kumina or Pocomania possession trances of Jamaica and to those of the 'voodoo' types of religion found in Roman Catholic areas of Afro-America, where the influence of Dahomeyan *vodun* is quite clear. However, it almost always takes a less complete form than these non-Christian varieties of possession and is better described as a degree of ecstasy or an alteration of consciousness. But it is very hard to make clear-cut distinctions. At one extreme of its manifestation in black Pentecostal services, the experience of the power of the Spirit can indeed take the form of seeming unconsciousness or the complete darkening of outward senses. At the other, the mundane extreme, religious ecstasy shades into joy, aesthetic pleasure and thanksgiving.

The Spirit manifests itself in many culturally distinct patterns of behaviour, referred to as 'getting in the Spirit' or 'being in the Spirit'. It may be expressed in sudden spasmodic jerks, intense 'shivering', peculiar arm and leg movements, walking around with upraised hands, crying, shouting ('Hallelujah!', 'Amen!', 'Glory!' or 'Jesus!'), dancing, running, jumping and even laughing. To 'dance in the Spirit', to 'jump in the Spirit', to 'sing in the Spirit', to 'move in the Spirit' and to 'speak in tongues' (glossolalia) are all culturally slanted, ecstatic spiritual reactions to the power of the Holy Spirit.

That most black Pentecostals firmly believe in the power of

the Spirit can be seen from the frequent accounts of spiritual experience outside church. Visions of lights and divine visitations are not uncommon. Some church-goers may at times receive a 'second-sight' vision of the hidden problems of others.

The pitch of spiritual experience during a church service is reached, however, via a collective act of worship involving much emotionally charged interaction and a striking and expressive use of sound. Such use of sound is characteristic of the oral tradition of Afro-America and is certainly not confined to the Churches. Martha Warren Beckwith, writing on oral folk culture in Jamaica (1929), aptly states that Jamaicans give expression to their 'inner life' through sound and motion. Striking and vibrant use of sound is found in many different black speech events, from verbal duelling (for instance, in the 'dozens' of black America), through black narrative style, to debate. Velma Pollard, writing on black story-telling in the Caribbean, states: 'In the folk milieu every narration is an unrehearsed dramatic presentation with varying orchestration' (Pollard, 1977). The Rastafarians are well aware of the special value of sound in Afro-Caribbean cultural life (see Jah Bones, 'Language and Rastafari', pp. 37–51 below).

Spiritual intensity too is generated by many speech events and has been commented on at some length by Kochman, for instance, who has examined the differences between black and white debating styles in America (Kochman, 1981). He found that whites tried to rein in their expressive or emotional impulses in debate, in contrast to blacks. In classroom discussion, he noted, not only were whites constrained by the high level of energy and spiritual intensity generated by blacks, but they were also worried that blacks could not manage such intense levels of interaction without losing control. However, for blacks the essential is that these internal forces are not repressed but both generated and controlled by the cultural speech event. In black church worship this spiritual intensity is seen as a step towards religious ecstasy, which, both released and controlled (as Kochman has it), appears in so-called secular contexts.

In this respect black church concerts, for instance, have much in common both with black church services and with secular black concerts. The audience have their common link, their cultural unity as black people, which profoundly affects and moulds every other aspect of the event, the Christian message of the lyrics aside. Indeed, it is accurate to say that gospel music differs from certain other types of black American music (significantly called 'Soul') only in that the latter speak of the love of another person rather than the love of Jesus. The audience respond to the performance and participate in it. According to their inner impulses and their appreciation of the performers, they stand, clap, urge on the artists ('Sing it!', 'That's it!', 'Yes!'). They frequently respond physically as well as vocally, swaying, moving rhythmically to the point of actually dancing. They react enthusiastically to particular phrasing (either choice of words or articulation, sung or spoken). Invariably this phrasing reveals an individualistic interpretation of black/'roots' aesthetics. Thus the performers and the audience together underline, or dig deeper into, the 'blackness' of the occasion, and they raise the emotional temperature. Energy is released and used, in a seemingly untiring, open-ended way, in a series of joint performances.

The black aesthetic enacted here is similar whether in church services, at church concerts or in completely secular, 'performance' contexts. In all of them the performers (including the audience) build to a high level of spiritual intensity. Moreover, this aesthetic, with its group interaction and its release of energies through sound and motion, suggests the African view of a spiritual universe of interactive forces.

The black Pentecostal Churches are a vital, flourishing and centrally important institution in the British black community – contrary to what one might conclude from their invisibility in the media and in academic publications. In their ability to organize and concentrate effort and resources they are unequalled in the community, and they continue to play a major role in the lives of many black people, young as well as old. In providing a spiritual anchor and a space to develop a satisfying black identity, they rival the Rastafarians. Again contrary to expectations perhaps, in their oral-spiritual culture, their ethnography of communication, their aesthetics and their world view the Churches claim a central place in black culture and show a clear debt to Africa. The oral accomplishment and the facility in exteriorizing one's thoughts that are associated with Afro-American cultures as a whole are nowhere seen more clearly than within the Churches. Let the Church roll on.

A Footnote on Creole

There is a tension between the use of Creole (Afro-Lingua or 'Nation Language') and of English in church services. Since the church is a public and respectable place, English, the language of public speaking and respectability, is the initial choice – or rather the target, since many older members can only edit out the more obvious markers of Creole rather than actually switch to English. But church services involve the congregation in sincere and often emotional self-revelation that favours Creole. Thus many of the Caribbean-born members will shift to Creole for the 'deeper' (that is, the essential) parts of the worship. Some speakers, indeed, may almost dispense with English and deliver an entire sermon, testimony or prayer in Creole, but most will begin in a more English idiom, leaving open the option of a shift.

Younger members – and those under 25 will almost certainly be British-born – generally use English throughout their worship but are able to shift style, including tempo, voice quality and phonology, according to the emotional temperature, very clearly marking their utterances as more black. This does not mean that they cannot speak a British form of Jamaican Creole – in the majority of instances they can (we believe, generalizing from our knowledge of the Churches in the West Midlands) and often very proficiently. These younger members are mostly female, and this is a significant factor. Young black women in Britain tend to use Creole in a more restricted range of situations than their male peers – in non-public utterances, in asides or in joking or emotional conversations, especially within an intimate circle (see, for example, 'London Jamaican and Black London English', Mark Sebba, pp. 149–67 below).

The proficient use of Creole by young Christians is particularly interesting, since some observers of the British black scene have concluded that this language is the badge of the 'Counter-Culture' and associate its use with a rebellious stance against white society. This is misleading. We might say by way of a corrective that the use of Creole shows an embracing of black cultural identity. Use of Creole to the exclusion of English shows an exclusive adherence to black (more specifically 'roots') identity, as in the case of some Rastas; use of Creole in a pointed way where it is not expected – in talking to teachers, for example – may show an aggressive, rebellious stance. Young black Christians do not typically take such a stance, and their lives are barely touched by what is normally referred to as the 'Counter-Culture', but they have instinctively chosen their own road to black cultural identity.

2

Proverbs of Jamaica

PASTOR L. A. JACKSON

Proverbs are an inherited oral literature. Sometimes they refer to longer fables, as in 'Follow-fashion monkey broke him neck' (from the Ashanti). Although younger people, especially the Rastas, make some use of proverbs, certain members of the older generation are living storehouses of them and use them vigorously. Black preachers, as we saw in the previous chapter, employ proverbs to express their meaning dramatically and memorably. Pastor Jackson, originally from Jamaica, gives his selection and comments on their use.

The following sayings are intended to teach awareness in all walks of life, especially to children. This awareness, it is hoped, will persist throughout their lifetime.

Chicken de go big u see it a them foot.
The size of the young chicken's feet shows whether or not it will grow up to be a fine fowl. The attitude of a young person speaks for his or her future.

Chicken da merry hawk de near.
Like the chicken who merrily scratches for food while the hawk hovers overhead, the child who plays heedlessly may not notice lurking perils. Too much pleasure can be dangerous.

Idle dogs worry sheep.
Similar to 'The devil finds work for idle hands': the mild and harmless are at risk from aggression born of idleness.

Simple straw blind eyes.
It is the small and apparently insignificant things that may hurt one for the rest of one's life. It is better to accept changes and difficulties than to ignore them, for one cannot guess at their consequences.

A drowning man catch after straw.
Someone who is in need will accept any help that is offered.

A naked man wear pickney shirt.
A naked man is happy to wear a boy's shirt: there is no place for pride when one is in need.

U can't catch Harry u catch em shirt.
If someone who has harmed you is out of reach, you take your revenge on the nearest person.

Fire under mus-mus tail em think a cool breeze.
Someone who cannot tell the difference between danger and pleasure will find himself in trouble. (Older children use this proverb to indicate to younger children that their behaviour is annoying.)

Do not set fire to fury.
Never fan the flames of a quarrel: try to make peace instead.

A no everyone got luck to carry goat over river.
It is not everyone who is lucky enough to take goats across the river. (Goats are generally afraid of water and resist most people's attempts to get them to ford a stream or river.) Good fortune is the prerogative of some: it is foolish to take chances on the assumption that one will succeed.

A no the same day leaf drop in a water it rotten.
You should beware of becoming involved in any secret actions, the consequences of which may not be immediately apparent but which may well come back to trouble you at a later time.

Stranger no know deep water.
You should be careful of becoming involved in other people's affairs unless you are absolutely sure that you know all the facts – especially where others' families are concerned.

Don't be like a running potato.
When a potato vine 'runs' it becomes incapable of bearing any potatoes. Hence if you are like a running potato, your life has become purposeless.

Empty barrel make the most noise.
Those who brag or bluster the most, generally cowards, are least likely to put their words into action.

Jack Panyar no ask fee feather em ask fee long life.
This saying encourages patience. The Jack Panyar is a small bird with short feathers. It asks for long life rather than feathers in the hope that with long life it will gain long feathers anyway.

Young dogs no know lion.
Children, like young dogs, are incapable of distinguishing what is safe from what is dangerous. They cannot tell whether something will be helpful or destructive.

Dogs lap sa 'Fee u, fee u.'
When dogs are drinking, or lapping, water they say, 'Your own, your own.' In other words, you should always make sure that you receive what you are due.

Dogs sweat but long hair cover it.
This refers to those who suffer but do not show it – for example, those who appear happy while concealing sorrow.

Dogs have many owners go to sleep without dinner.
If you spread your loyalties too widely, you will not be rewarded. More specifically, if you make a habit of trying to eat at your friends' homes, you may find that you end up not eating at all.

Play with puppy, puppy lick u mout.
If you are too familiar with those subordinate or junior to yourself, you will find that you lose their respect, which will be bad for both parties.

Where dogs are not wanted, bones are not provided.
If you are greeted with this saying, you will certainly understand that you are not welcome!

There are more dogs than bones.
This saying is always used by people in authority, who respond to requests for more by telling those beneath them that there is not enough to go round.

You are cat and dog.
This is said to people when they are unable to agree or are quarrelling.

The dog that takes in a bone will carry one out.
This is a warning against listening to gossips or tale-bearers. If they talk to you about other people, you can be sure that they will be talking about you when out of your hearing.

See and blind, hear and deaf.
Another way of advocating discretion: whatever you see or hear, it is best to mind your own business.

Play with fire u get burn.
Do not trifle with danger. Make sure that you know whom you are dealing with when you become involved with others' affairs, and do not take risks.

Too much rats never dig good holes.
This is analogous to 'Too many cooks spoil the broth.' There are many situations where a large number of people will do a job less efficiently than fewer. The saying also implies that where large numbers are involved it is difficult to keep plans secret.

Less Turke less yaws.
This is a warning against inviting disobedience or intransigence. The fewer people you involve in any endeavour, the less likely you are to enlist those who are a bad influence.

If duck won't left pond, pond will left duck.
You cannot expect things to go on forever unchanged. If you do not make efforts to change your interests and friends, you will find that you have been left behind. Essentially, the message is that one should always be prepared to adapt when circumstances change.

Cattle won't hear woe, em neck belongs to butcher.
If a child does not listen to advice, it will soon find itself in trouble.

U can't stay on cow[s]kin cuss cow.
You cannot both rely on others to make life comfortable for you and abuse their friendship and generosity by criticizing or presuming on them.

Cow horn has never been too heavy for its head.
We are never required to deal with more than we can manage, so it is incumbent on us to accept our responsibilities without complaint.

The humblest calf suck the most milk.
It is the neediest who justly receive the most attention.

Cow sa mas-sa work na done.
Do what you can today, but do not worry about leaving some work for another day. If a cow can recognize that its master's work cannot all be done in one day, then so should you.

Stay on the crooked and cut strait.
Even when you are in difficulties, try to make the best of things and aim, in the long run, to achieve what you want.

Don't be a panyar mashate (machete).
A panyar machete has two edges: don't dissimulate – say what you mean and mean what you say.

Hard ears pickney dead a sun hot.
Children who are disobedient and ignore the advice of their elders by turning 'hard ears' to them will find themselves in trouble when the going gets rough.

U don't know the use of halfa knife until it lost.
A warning to enjoy and appreciate things from day to day, as we often do not realize their value fully until they are no longer available.

Want it, want it, can't get. Have it, have it, don't want.
Similar to the preceding proverb: we should enjoy what we have, as the things we take for granted may be much envied by others less fortunate.

Finger stink, u can't cut-e throw wae.
Just as you cannot cut off a sore finger but must treat it until it is better, so there are certain problems from which you cannot shrink: they will remain until you do something about them.

Tiger grow old it eat cockroach.
Similar to 'Beggars can't be choosers': we should accept with gratitude what is offered to us when we cannot provide for ourselves.

Spit in the sky, it falls in your face.
If you deliberately flout convention, courtesy or propriety, you will very quickly experience retribution of one kind or another – things have a habit of turning sour on you when you disregard the sensibilities of others or act dishonestly.

3

Language and Rastafari

JAH BONES

Rasta has been described as a fashion or as the millennial dreaming of the powerless. Jah Bones describes Rasta as power- (or 'powah'-) ful. The word recurs in this book. Rasta's mission in Britain has been to accumulate cultural power through language. At the heart of all this lies the word and sound /I/ and the /I-an-I/ or commonality of human beings, members one of another. Despite being regarded by some as bizarre, Rasta speaks to the modern human condition, while having a particular relevance to many blacks in Britain and elsewhere.

Of recent times there has been a keen interest in the Rastafarian Movement, and this, in my view, is due to the fact that the Movement is truly international as opposed to being a one-island phenomenon. More, it is reality. Today there are substantial Rastafarian communities not only in Jamaica but in all of the former English-speaking islands of the Caribbean, as well as in territories that were ruled by the French, Dutch and Spanish; in the UK, the USA, Canada, Africa, New Zealand, Australia; on the European continent and in South America. Thus a great many people in all these countries are asking, either in verbal exchanges or in the literature: What is Rasta? What is the lifestyle? Are Rastas friendly or hostile? Why do Rastas want to be different? Are Rastas misled myth-makers, or are they informed reality-creators?

This reaction is normal in a situation where people feel threatened because they perceive strangers. The Rastas are perceived as strangers because the typical Western personality is an ego-image of the self. It is rather difficult for most (if not all) ego-types to perceive a person who does not reflect the standard or normal ego-type as anything other than a stranger. Depicted as a stranger by the standard ego-type person, the Rasta becomes the 'other', a contradiction to the standard ego-type person, who is dominated by a philosophy which can be characterized as selfishness. And the type form or structure of this personality is real because the key values of the philosophy are instinctive. That is why many non-Rastas are defensive in their initial contacts with Rastafarians. To them Rastas represent the invasion of strangers (a host of 'others') in highly valued philosophical and behavioural terrain.

However, it must be said that in relation to Western culture and all its implications the Rastafarians do indeed represent a great deal that is different. For example, in the context of religion Rasta theology or doctrine is different; the dredlocks hairstyle is different; Rasta cuisine is different, with its emphasis on that which is natural or 'Ital' (vital); Rasta music is different because it is a fundamental drum music with singing, emphasizing a collective effort as opposed to the egoistic, stardom-seeking singing that typifies popular music. The Rastas' music, called *nyahbingi*, is very powerful indeed. Not strangely, it is observed that the Rastas speak differently. They are gradually putting together the rudiments of a peculiar language. I say 'peculiar' because this language is strictly Rastafarian, and the more it develops, the more distinct it will become.

This essay will, it is hoped, sketch for readers the basic elements of the rudiments of the Rasta language or 'livalek'; explain, as far as space allows, words of importance, in terms of their structure, role and meaning; and, by implication, demonstrate the usefulness and validity of the 'Afro-Lingua'. This term came into use as early as the 1960s. It is the one that I like to use because it depicts the Rasta feeling for language better than the rest. For a people who were shorn of a substantial amount of institutional power, cultural power became the only objective in the area of socio-human relationships. Hence the Rastas soon understood that the possession of linguistic power was realizable and that it would be good because it would be helpful. Language is very important in human beings' lives. It enables us to communicate; it is the vehicle for our thoughts. In that sense it is always pregnant with a variety of coded messages that are characterized essentially by sounds. To the Rastas, then, words are really sounds that acquire meaning and significance in relation to social power or structure. But before we say more about that, let us turn our attention to the nature and role of Rastafari as a way of life ('livity') and as a doctrine.

Rastafari: Origins and Growth

What follows is a brief outline of the origins and growth of the Rastafarian Movement. Here we are concerned particularly with tracing certain key trends and marking certain crucial generalities, as distinct from dealing with units, figures and details.

It is safe to say that the pressures of certain spiritual, historical and social forces increased to the point where they gave birth to Jah Rastafari Movement. It was in 1930 that Negus Tafari, who was also Rastafari, was crowned King of Kings and Lord of Lords, Emperor of Ethiopia. This act, and what it symbolized, was all that was needed for Brother Leonard Howell, and a few others like Archibald Dunkley, Robert Hinds and Joseph Hibbert, to take on the duty of spreading the word that the Christ had returned. The Emperor of Ethiopia, Haile Selassie I, is to his new-found disciples the King of Israel or of the Jews: God's chosen people. By this time the new disciples were convinced that the African people, black people, were the true and original Jews and Israelites, whom God had chosen to save as long as they kept serving him by obeying his laws and manifesting his will. This conception is fundamentally spiritual or religious but is intimately related to racial, political and economic realities.

How did the new disciples arrive at this conception? Personal experience, an adequate knowledge and understanding of things in the world, and reading, especially of the Bible, played a very important part in the crystallization of the conception.

In terms of the significance of the new religious awareness, the Bible (the King James version) was seen as the most objective and respected source of authenticity, not least because it is the authority of religious validity for the Christian population. Yet when the Rastas validated their claim or corroborated their proposition with reference to the Bible, this was held to be mischievous and wrong. By insisting on Africa and blackness the early Rastas were not only defining a racial awareness; they were also defining a national awareness. The new disciples accepted Marcus Garvey's exhortation in full: 'Africa for the Africans, those at home and those abroad'.

Holding firm to such an emotive slogan meant that Rastas had to reject assimilation and, as a consequence, appeared more and more a segregationist movement. The establishment of the Rasta community at Pinnacle, in the parish of St Catherine, Jamaica, reflected in a practical way the segregationist tendency. Pinnacle lasted for about fifteen years. The Jamaican Government demolished Pinnacle in 1954, thus forcing its occupants to seek refuge in adjoining parishes, but especially Kingston, the capital of Jamaica. The refugees settled in areas of West Kingston like Trench Town, Rose Town, Back-O-Wall and Ackee-Walk, where they soon started making their presence felt. By 1956 the Rastas from Pinnacle were gaining converts to the Faith at a rapid rate. The number of Rastas who were forced out of Pinnacle was substantial: it was reported to be some 500 to 700. Even if only 400 had finally settled in Kingston, that would have been a large number to have in the midst of dispossessed and underprivileged ghetto youths. I myself was one of those youths who accepted the Rasta Faith, as in it I saw something to identify with; it gave me a feeling of belonging and a brighter perception of the future because it helped me to understand the past in a way that was impossible before.

The Ethiopian Land Grant of 1955, which was to be administered by the Ethiopian World Federation Incorporated (EWF Inc.), established in 1937, gave a boost to the flagging fortunes of the Federation and at the same time provided tangible hopes for those dispossessed who desired to return to Ethiopia. Rastas in Jamaica were becoming so restless and vociferous that in 1958 and 1960 two false moves were made concerning repatriation. The antagonisms, conflicts and confrontations of the period resulted in the commissioning, by the Government of the day, of a team of social scientists from the University of the West Indies to study the condition and needs of the Rastafarians in Kingston (Nettleford et al., 1960).

The report was basically favourable to Rastas. It blamed society for creating and keeping in existence the conditions that Rastas vehemently abhor. It affirmed Rastafari as a legitimate way of life, and it even espoused the idea of repatriation. As a consequence a fact-finding mission went to five African countries in 1961 to see how repatriation could best be effected. The mission returned with little promise or hope of a quick return to Africa for the Rastas. The outcome was not surprising. A great many Rastas had distrusted the move anyway; to them the mission was like an exercise in public relations designed to forestall an impending hostile confrontation arising from the Rastafarians' need for repatriation and society's need to prove that repatriation was impractical. But the movement of Rasta could not be stopped, for Rastafari was destined to expand beyond the shores of Jamaica.

Rastafari in Britain: 1960 to the Present

Between 1950 and 1962 hundreds of thousands of immigrants from the Caribbean islands migrated to Britain. As a result of the Second World War, Britain needed labourers to work in factories, in transport, in hospitals. The Afro-Caribbean black people fitted the bill, and Britain became a home from home. The number of Rastas who came to Britain in the earlier years was very small. (The overwhelming majority of Rastafarians were totally against emigrating to the UK.) However, numbers notwithstanding, the task of establishing Rastafari in Britain was a challenge to the few as well as to the many.

Gatherings and reasonings of Rastafarians in the UK took place at Rastas' homes, as there was nowhere else to meet. For the early Rastas of Britain it was very noticeable that the *nyahbingi* was missing, and that was a serious deprivation. The *ganja* weed was in good supply and that was always obtained. The doctrine of Rastafari was, and is, the same for Rastas in Britain as for Rastas in Jamaica. The one great difference is that Britain is not a tropical country and appears poorly endowed by nature. Thus whereas the Rastas of Jamaica lived with the conception that they must harmonize with nature, the Rastas of Britain found that they were protected from it by artificial means. In Britain it is difficult to reach nature because it is apparently or actually remote. At the same time most Rastas in Britain, during the 1960s as now, felt that they stood a better chance of returning to Africa from the UK.

It did not take Rastas in the UK long to realize that a great purpose lay behind the establishment of Rastafari in Britain. The reasoning went like this. Since Britain claimed to be the 'mother country' because of its former role as a colonial power, it was only logical, in relation to the development of forces, that Rastas were domiciled in the heart of Babylon, sitting by the River Thames and weeping and singing as they all remembered Zion – thus proving that the Rastafarians are the ancient Israelites of old. Zion is Ethiopia. Babylon is a fallen empire, and European imperialism is the reincarnated Babylon, which is destroying itself. Rastas saw that they were chosen to be God's 'watchmen' here on earth. Babylon cannot contradict the Rasta because the Bible is true.

The 1970s saw a great increase in the growth of Rastafari in the UK. Many young people came to Britain from the Caribbean as families sought to unite their members. Between 1960 and 1974 hundreds of thousands of them must have arrived. These young people, along with their parents, were to experience a great deal of social and psychological disturbance. They were uprooted from humble rural and urban surroundings and planted in an highly industrialized society, the like of which they had not countenanced before their arrival in Britain. Shocks, stresses and strains were counteracted by music, dancing, fun and laughter. But some young people demanded a more thoroughgoing system of counteraction. They were looking at the situation in a more serious light.

The establishment in about 1971 of the Ethiopian World Federation (EWF) Inc., in Ladbroke Grove, West London, was welcomed by young London Rastas who were seeking a more formal togetherness. In 1973 the Ethiopian Orthodox Church was also established in Ladbroke Grove. It was the Federation that brought the Church to Britain. Thus the early Federation members became the nucleus of the original membership of the Church. The Twelve Tribes of Israel organization of Jamaica established a UK group in 1973 in South London. Over the years Twelve Tribes has grown steadily and now has members all over Britain.

From time to time Rastas, whether in Britain or Jamaica, form smallish organizations and associations. The intention is to bring all Rastas together. In 1981 a Rastafarian conference was held in Brixton, London, which resulted in a commitment by the represented groups that the EWF Inc. should be revived and that it should serve as the umbrella organization of a united Rasta movement in Britain. But because of regional bias, organizational disputes, personality clashes, lack of clarity of concepts and philosophies and even lack of discipline, the anticipated progress has not been made.

Yet, slowly but surely, Rastas are organizing themselves all over – in the West Indies, Britain, Africa, North America, New Zealand and elsewhere. Rastas have stood the test of

time and action, so progress is inevitable. The Rastafarians
have already made progress – a great deal of progress, in fact.
One has just got to look at the way in which the Rasta way
has changed many aspects of life: food and cooking, music
and dance, religious awareness, business and employment,
and culture and behaviour, an area where language is very
important. And for the rest of this essay language will be our
main topic as we analyse how and why the Rastafarians have
made such important changes in so fortified an area of cultural domination.

Afro-Lingua: the Basis of a Rasta Language

In Jamaica, where the Rastafarians originated, the English
language is the official language. But it is not spoken by the
majority of Jamaicans, who are African descendants. From
the time of slavery until now, the majority of Jamaicans have
spoken a language drawn from African and English words
but delivered with African sounds. When the words and the
sound go together people call it Patois or 'Patwa', which is
more Afro-Caribbean or Afro-Lingua. Some people call the
language broken English; Rastas prefer to say that it is
broken African because 'broken English' suggests that one is
not liberating oneself from colonialism. That is exactly why I
prefer to use Afro-Lingua.

Patois was established long before Rastas emerged in
Jamaica. Every boy and girl of peasant stock was fully socialized in the unofficial language; one could not be literate in it
because it was not taught in any school. Patois had to be the
language of the newly emerging Rastafarians. From an early
period, possibly when Pinnacle was at its peak, Rastas sought
to elevate the Jamaican Patois by introducing both a strong
emphasis on sound and regular inflections in words and
phrases in order to accentuate rhythm and style. It was not
long after the Pinnacle refugees had hit Kingston that the
style of speech of the Kingston ghettos was influenced by the
Rastafarians. The ghetto youths realized that the Rastas were
making Patois more interesting. Those Jamaicans who were

not Rastas were somewhat ashamed of Patois. They spoke it only because they were unable to do 'better'. But the Rastas felt that the language was the African people's own, that they should be proud of it and should set about improving it.

All Rastas have certain crucial values and properties in common. Thus it is not surprising that the Rastafarians of Britain are genuinely proud of Afro-Lingua. The young black people of Britain who are into black consciousness and cultural awareness are keen to speak Afro-Lingua because it reinforces their awareness and gives them hope where otherwise there would be despair. By the time Rasta took off in Britain the basis, structure and content of Afro-Lingua were already established and fully operative. For the black youth of Britain who wanted (and still wants) an alternative cultural system – which, by definition, means an alternative society – the Rastafarian life and philosophy was the answer. There is a substantial number of black people in Britain today, and the Rasta community has its fair numbers within that; Afro-Lingua will be spoken in Britain as long as Afro-Caribbean people and Rastafarians live there. There is no sign at all that the black youth of Britain is denouncing and renouncing Afro-Lingua: on the contrary, all the signs are pointing in the opposite direction. Admittedly, I have observed that the young people who were born in Britain are responding differently to racism and despair – differently, that is, from those who were born in the Caribbean but have grown up in Britain, who tend to identify with Caribbean culture faster. This is logical because their affinity with the West Indies is stronger. The black youths who were born in Britain are keen to understand Afro-Caribbean culture because they are partly socialized into it (in so far as it holds in their families), but they are less keen to practise it as a rule.

Some Basic Words in Afro-Lingua

First, let us consider certain fundamental principles. Rastas see the English language as decadent, or at least stagnant, just as they hold that Patois is stagnant. Rastas think that one reason for linguistic stagnation is that the English language is a social-class language. From this it follows that the language reflects all the biases and negative features of the class of which it is a product. The Rastas discover as well that the language has racial biases that complement the class biases; this is unacceptable to the African people who are fighting for liberation from imperial and colonial domination.

For example, black is depicted as bad or disastrous. 'A black day' means that on a particular day things have gone badly for the whites; they have suffered a loss or have done badly in an important affair. 'A black sheep in the family' means the worst or most detested member of a family. One sees, quite clearly, that black is associated with the devil and hell and with death. At the same time the assumption is that white is good, right, pure and everything that is opposite to bad. But in reality, of course, this is not true. There is no doubt that the black–white opposition is racial and racist.

Let us look at the letter I. We are told that in the context of grammar 'I' is the first-person pronoun and that the latter takes the place of a noun. We also know that other personal pronouns (you, he, she, they) are second- and third-person pronouns. Rastas say this is a reflection of a class society, where the blacks are seen as 'you', 'they' and so forth but never as 'I'. But since 'I' is the first person singular, 'I' is Jah Rastafari, Haile Selassie I, the one and only. Jah is black, so it follows that 'I' is black. Black, Jah and 'I' are now interchangeable terms, each meaning the same as the other.

Each Rastaman is a 'Jahman'; equally each 'Jahman' is an 'I-man'. Hence an 'I-man' is also a 'you-man' (or 'human'). Now the 'I-man' is different from the 'you-man' or 'me-man' because he is the first person. So since Rasta is 'I', a plurality of Rastas become 'I-n-I'. Thus 'I-n-I overstand Babylon style, right now it naw seh notten' means 'We understand the Babylon style of doing things, but at the moment that is saying nothing.'

Take 'overstand'. This word was invented to contradict 'understand'. We know that 'understand' is a verb, a doing or action word. The question now arises: How can one act in an 'under' situation? If it happens that one gets some action going, then it won't be easy. In English there are antonyms, which oppose synonyms. If 'understand' is a synonym for 'comprehend', where is its opposite or antonym? In the English language 'overstand' is not the opposite of 'understand'. However, in Afro-Lingua it *is* the opposite, whereas 'understand' is 'downposit' or 'underposit'. To 'overstand' something is to comprehend it or to obtain an 'overview'.

Before we go further let us say something more about 'I' as a concept and as a word. The Rastafarians seek at all times to use I- as a prefix for most nouns and verbs. For instance, creation becomes 'Iration', beginning 'Iginin', respect 'Ispect' or 'Ispek', control 'Itroll', meditate 'Iditate', reconcile 'Iconcile' and so forth. As we have seen, I is the premier letter and sound as well as word. Thus it is only appropriate to prefix the words with I- .

Some English words end in -ment; these are eliminated at all times. The basis for this is that Rasta reject 'men' and deal only with 'man'. To Rastas the word 'man' is like 'sheep': the singular form is the same as the plural. 'Man', in Rasta, is good, and this is shown by his constant obedience to Jah Rastafari, Haile Selassie I. 'Men', on the other hand, is bad. Rastas claim biblical support for their proposition that 'man' is different from 'men' and that this is illustrated by the fact that men are many, varied and confused, but man is one who is motivated by love and harmony. Listen to St Matthew 26:24: 'The Son of man goeth as it is written of him: but woe unto that man by whom the Son of man is betrayed! it had been good for that man if he had not been born.' Rastas always say that I-n-I were born man but some man fall from grace by sinning and become men. 'Peter answered and said unto him, Though all men shall be offended because of thee, yet will I never be offended' (St Matthew 26:33). This is so because Peter is a man and refuses to descend to the level of men. Again, St Mark 3:28: 'Verily I say unto you, All sins shall be forgiven unto the sons of men, and blasphemies wherewith soever they shall blaspheme' (men reproduce themselves because after a time they inherit men behaviour).

Take a word like 'appreciate'. This is supposed to express a feeling of gratitude and satisfaction, but the suffix -ate has a hostile sound. That is a contradiction in terms of morality, sound and power – that is, socio-cultural vibrations. I-n-I prefer to say 'apprecilove', for that is the moral principle and relates better to satisfaction and gratitude. 'Ital' means vital; 'Irie' is like saying 'how-d'e-do'; 'Isis' is praises; 'mantal' is mental. A word like 'congregation' could easily be switched to 'congreman' or 'congrelove' or 'Igregaman', though one generally hears Rastas say 'gathering' (only it would be spelt 'gadarin', Afro-Lingua style).

In Rasta everything can be classed as 'dred' (my spelling). 'Dred' is power or 'powah'. It is great, hard as opposed to soft, and, of course, anything that is frightening or fearful is 'dred'. 'Jah' is Father and Son. I father's name is 'Jah', and I Son's name is 'Jah'. Whenever a Rasta says 'lion' he is talking of the strength which man possesses, plus the lion as king of the jungle (whereas man is king of the nations). Jah Rastafari is Haile Selassie I, great and 'tundarable' (thunderable). The Rasta talk or 'livalek' (dialect) is filled with words that are taken from basic Jamaican 'Patwa', which has many left-over African words. Further, Amharic words are penetrating Rasta language. Words like 'wa-da-da' (love), 'tenaestilin' (greetings), 'issat' (fire) and others are regularly used and are very potent because they colour the talk with exotic designs.

Words, Sounds and 'Powah'

According to Rasta doctrine and reasoning, a language must have great significance in terms of its words, sounds and 'powah', which means 'power'. Language must also relate to manifestations: it represents the ideal and the real. Language relates everything that is seen, heard, felt, imagined, known. The 'powah' in every reasoning, argument and discussion must be 'Irated' or vibrated 'thru' words and sounds. Sounds are very important because they allow words to reach people with an impact, so that they are drawn to their attention. It is crucial that people 'overstand' words for what they really are; 'thru' sounds they will achieve the 'powah' of wisdom or 'wisman', knowledge or 'Iridge' and 'overstanding'.

The vibration ('Iration') that words and sounds generate among human beings is not seriously checked by many people. Rastafarians feel the 'Iration'; therefore they check deeply for it. They also seek consciously to generate more and more 'Iration', hence the long hours spent in reasoning sessions. This becomes a highly valued activity, an on-going process, so that more and more 'powah' is accumulated. The 'powah' is what gives Rasta strength and makes him formidable. Like his father, Rasta is a conquering lion.

As a language Afro-Lingua does not need grammar and rules because it relies on improvisation, quickwittedness and skill at manipulating words. Within the bounds of 'Iration' (that is, creativity) it is a free language because it allows for free as opposed to restricted use. In the later part of the 1950s, when the groundwork of the language was being laid, it was put forward that the Rasta alphabet could not have A as the first letter but rather I. I-n-I would say that A, B, C, etc., is wrong. In Rasta it would have to be I, C, A, B, etc. For Rastas would say that all languages are invented and created by people; it therefore follows that since people have eyes and they see things (some more than others), it is quite reasonable to build on the foundation of the real: I, C, etc.

In Rasta 'powah' transcends rules. I-n-I are earnestly seeking 'powah thru di I'. Since Rastafari is based on nature ('Iration'), it is only appropriate to put 'I' first in cultural 'Ifares' or affairs. One knows then that one has a secure foundation.

Language and Control

One of the key aspects of language is its role as a control mechanism. A highly restricted language is elitist in character, so it reflects all sorts of biases and prejudices. Rastas are saying that the language of the former colonial masters (say, English) is biased and prejudiced, reflecting the values and morals of the colonial masters' conduct and behaviour.

Languages transmit values and standards that are learned by recipients through social conditioning and the internalization of the same values and standards. Socialization takes its ugliest form when people are forced to adopt other languages at the expense of their own.

The Rasta language is non-colonial because it is based on truths and rights. To Rastafarians the black people have words, sounds, as a gift from Jah. But words and sounds can create ('crelove') 'powah' only when they are related to truth and rights. Liberation can be gained only when a people possesses power by knowing its rights and seeking the truth. It is very important that people should know that imperialism's 'divide and rule' relies heavily on using languages as a device for social control.

The British, for example, used their language as they used guns, money, law, religion, politics or anything else: as a weapon in the battles and wars of domination and foreign rule. I-n-I must realize that if change is to be made (and it is being made), it is necessary to break the sequence of social conditioning. It is important to see that the issue of social awareness and the identification of blackness relate to language as much as to anything else. Since the conditioning process has to be reversed, it is vital that people should start checking language hard.

It is the cultural and linguistic 'downpression' or oppression that Rastas 'downpose' or oppose. It goes without saying that people cannot be free when they are controlled. It is a contradiction to say to people that they are free when they are controlled by a subtle thing like language. When, as black people, you speak as a 'mother' tongue a language that characterizes black as bad and purely negative, then it is time to take stock, especially when white is portrayed as good at all times.

Freedom and language are closely related. Now, if people cannot argue their rights, cannot talk the truth and cannot argue for justice, then they cannot be free. For freedom (or 'freeman') to be realized, I-n-I must know that the medium and the expression must be one and the same thing. When the medium (or language) is different from the expression, then the whole scene is substantially negative. Black language and black concepts must correspond, must harmonize. That is why Rastas are trying so hard to 'crelove' a language that is in full correspondence with their concepts.

Whether Rastas live in Britain, Jamaica, Trinidad, the USA or wherever, it is imperative that I-n-I learn African languages – there are enough to choose from. It would be a great advantage were I-n-I to do so; it would serve to facilitate I-n-I 'settleman' in Africa!

4

Reggae Deejaying and Jamaican Afro-Lingua

JAH BONES

As with other chapters in this volume, this chapter emphasizes the spread of the Caribbean culture in Britain and the accelerated development of its forms. This happened when the 'roots' culture became urbanized in Jamaica and (at about the same time) in Britain. Rasta used, influenced and was advanced by this change. Reggae and its technology in turn disseminated Rasta and its language. As Jah Bones says, Creole (Afro-Lingua) needs transmitting agencies like literature and music in order to flourish, and these are available in reggae and deejaying. A number of points emerge that are central to this deceptively informal but questing culture: the push for recognition (so successful that reggae sells internationally), joint participation or call-and-response and the sense of an informed creativity from which others can learn.

In this chapter I shall be talking about reggae music and Afro-Lingua, the Jamaican 'roots' language. I shall seek to do this by looking at the music and the language in its homeland, Jamaica, and then comparing and contrasting that with the developing Afro-Jamaican cultural situation in Britain, where there is a huge Jamaican community, which has been in that country since the Second World War. By comparing and contrasting the cultural realities of the two Jamaican communities, at home and abroad, I intend to demonstrate, in the

process, the strength of the very interesting, but little understood, Jamaican cultural styles. But, in this case, the strength
can only be revealed when the role, value and character are
revealed for what they really are in terms of the practical
purpose of the cultural heritage of a dynamic and vibrant
people.

It is by now undisputed that Jamaican reggae music is the
most effective carrier of Jamaica's cultural styles, which are
fighting a battle for recognition and acceptance. As I understand the Jamaican problems, they are more to do with
recognition and legality than with anything else. The problems of recognition and acceptance notwithstanding, however, the Jamaican people have persisted in cultural creations
that have served to catch the world's notice, and on a very
serious level too. Make no mistake, cultural inventions – for
that is truly what they are – like reggae music, Rasta religion
and Afro-Lingua command world interest and respect. No
doubt, this reality has been facilitated by the Jamaican and
Caribbean communities living in certain foreign countries:
(the UK, the USA, Canada) and frequenting others in Europe,
Africa and elsewhere.

A close look at the second and third generations of blacks
in Britain especially reveals very clearly the profound and
lasting nature of the Jamaican culture. (I emphasize Jamaica
more than the West Indies or the Caribbean because I
believe that the Jamaican culture absolutely dominates the
English-speaking Caribbean.) It was thought by politicians,
academics, priests, social relations engineers that because
Jamaican culture was fluid and nebulous it would die off;
consequently, all blacks from Jamaica and the Caribbean
would be nothing but British through and through. But this
has not happened. Jamaican culture has proved to be much
more substantial, structured and lasting than was previously
thought. The fact that Jamaican culture is a synthesis of
African tribal cultures and English or British culture does
not invalidate it at all. It is safe to say that all existing
cultures, no matter how proud or old, are a synthesis of
what has gone before or what has been forced on a society.

Adaptation and assimilation of cultures have been practised since antiquity. I do not think that the genesis of a culture determines its validity and acceptance; recognition comes through use, value and popularity.

Music and Language

Some people, in common with Professor Marshall McLuhan, believe that the medium is the message; in the reggae business dealers and customers think that it is specifically the music which is the message and that message is strictly delivered in Jamaican Patois or what I prefer to call Afro-Lingua. A people's music must be expressed through their language if they are to relate their feelings of joy, sorrow, hope or gratitude. The social nature of behaviour is such that people seek to identify with and relate to what they see and know to be uniquely theirs. The Jamaican Patois is a Creole language, by that I mean that it is a mixture of more than two languages, which came into being as a result of socio-cultural interaction and intercourse over time. It is a fact that this language is spoken by the overwhelming majority of Jamaicans. In most cases this is the only language they know. As I have said elsewhere (Bones, 1979), the English language like the English religion (Anglicanism), is a class language and is therefore spoken by only a tiny minority of Jamaicans. This may surprise most people, but it is the truth.

In music, singing plays a very important role. Singing conveys messages and feelings that cannot be conveyed by pure instrumentation. Singing and talking are related social behaviours. They rely on words, sound and power in order to acquire definition, structure and relevance, in order to obtain response and a sense of commonality. For a people singing and talking share the same language and thus all the linguistic symbols that go with such a language. In fact, with some people it is difficult to tell when they are singing from when they are talking. This would be truer of people with a more traditional civilization, where language is not rule-dominated but is relatively free from proscriptive rules and is more guided in its expression by rhythm and style expressed through sounds. The one, the rule-dominated language is meant to be objective, precise and relatively unemotional; the other is meant to be subjective, extensive and relatively emotional. This description holds well when one looks closely at what reggae music is offering – the way which it has breached the language barrier, widened the horizon of word, sound and, not least, bridged the gap between singing and talking, music and language. For reggae, most definitely, the music and the language are one and the same thing. The message can't be different because it's one sound, one word and one mouth, people, culture and all else that related to the people of reggae and Afro-Lingua.

From the times of slavery until now the Afro-Jamaican people, who are the roots and bastion of Jamaican society, have always sought to live as one. However, opposing forces attempted to repress that desire, so that cherished expression of oneness had to be postponed until social conditions changed sufficiently.

The 1950s and 1960s saw a period of radically changed social conditions. That era heralded a substantially greater measure of cultural freedom and movement. That, in fact, was the era of the birth of sound systems and, later, the birth of the Jamaican music business and industry. Prior to the advent of dance-hall music, when music was provided by a band (combo) or a smallish orchestra or, later, sound systems, Afro-Jamaicans would make and play music in yards on occasions like celebrations, ritualistic mourning of the dead, religious festivals and services or personal thanksgiving, when an individual seeks to offer gratitude to the Creator and to ask for blessing. But music by sound system is symbolic of an urbanized take-over of the Jamaican cultural lifestyle. The rural predominance had to give way because electricity is the sole source of energy or power for music by sound system. Before the advent of sound systems and electricity the people themselves were the only source of power and energy. Paradoxically, though, the advent of electricity and sound systems did not serve to rob the people of anything.

Even though it could be said that the sound system deperso-
nalized popular fun and dance music in one sense, in another
it could be said that deejays – disc jockeys, professional
players of records for public entertainment – rescued the
sound system from the drift towards alienating the maker of
music from those who were entertained by it. The deejays
have arisen to atone, as it were, for the sins of electrification
and the mass production of plastic discs that give the music a
faceless but beguiling attraction, as innocent as it is meant to
tranquillize.

It is my contention that the emergence of reggae music,
with its overt dependence on electrification and vinyl plastic
discs, marked the beginning of the urban ascendancy in
popular music and talk. Before the advent of the sound
system and its by-products popular culture was rural-domi-
nated. That is, people had to relate to the rural areas and
their communities when they sought cultural definitions in
areas such as language, religion, music, folklore or whatever.
But the musical revolution changed all that to a considerable
extent. After a time most Jamaicans wanted to dance like the
Kingstonians; they wanted to talk like them, sing like them
and, in fact, do everything like them. (Other areas of the
media, like television, helped to promote urban cultural
dominance over the rural areas, but the musical contribution
is what caused the change to be revolutionary in type.) Thus
reggae music has served to transform many poor youths'
lives, gaining for them a respectable livelihood and sometimes rocketing them to stardom and world fame.

Reggae music, through the deejays especially, has served to
enrich Afro-Lingua enormously. (Actually, the Rastafari
Movement has done even more to revolutionize Jamaican
cultural realities than reggae music because it is the chief
source of inspiration for reggae artists; but here we're concerned with music and language.) The music reinforces the
language and the other way round. Now the reggae deejays
are a great source of linguistic originality; they are also the
accepted authority on that which is legitimate or otherwise in
the language. And now reggae singers are being widely

influenced by the deejay trend in that they are utilizing the 'singjay' technique, which is to sing-talk, so that they are coming closer to Afro-Lingua all the time and moving away from English pronunciation because otherwise the words are not relevant to the music; everything must be strictly roots.

Reggae Deejaying in Jamaica

The reggae deejay was destined to be an important aspect of the reggae business. Sound systems needed attendants or operators, just as they needed owners – a sound system is such that it needs a group of workers to make it operable. Among any group of workers (or 'posse' or 'massive', as they are currently called) the deejay takes pride of place. He is the one that the dance crowds focus on, and if he has a charismatic personality and sufficient talent and is professionally skilled, then there is no stopping him. Swiftly such a person rises to fame, is talked about, is seen as a local hero, acquires contacts, wields influence and is well placed to transcend poverty if ambitious and balanced. A good deejay needs a good sound system and vice versa. But what does a deejay do? In the early times a deejay would operate the 'set', as a 'sound' is called, which means he would select the records and tune the amplifier so as to obtain the tone, pitch and rhythm of the amplified music. This practice continued during the 1950s. Around 1959 a famous deejay named Count Machuky – he was actually the number one deejay for the Sir Coxsone sound system, then Jamaica's foremost sound – started what was then called 'toasting' over the microphone. From the earliest times the deejays would possess a microphone, although it would be used only for announcing information to the dance crowd. But Machuky changed that. He had the idea that the deejay could use the microphone to harmonize the crowd, amuse the people and relieve the monotony of the non-stop churning of electric and plastic. The sound system had replaced the intimacy of the dance band days, when those who produced the music were real and live.

Count Machuky, as all good pioneers, felt that something was missing. In all reasonableness, he sensed the absence of a personal involvement in the music he was held to be producing. Could it be his and/or the people's non-involvement in the production of the music that was being played? With the music on the vinyl disc there is no room at all for improvisation or a changing pattern of improvisation over a particular rhythm track. Whatever is recorded in the studios is what you will always hear once it is recorded. But the deejay can replay the tune two or three times and vary his toasting as many times. Thus, Machuky, knowingly or otherwise, brought back an element of personal involvement at the produce-and-play level of the sound-system music and, even more to the point, by so doing created an opening for musical improvisation, which was all but lost in the neat packaging of a people's music.

Count Machuky was 'hip'. He would seek to release his otherwise pent-up emotions by using jiving phrases like, 'Skip and dip and shake your hip', 'Dig this live jive, from me to you and you to me.' Of course, he would say things on behalf of his sound, Sir Coxsone Downbeat, champion sound of all Jamaica at the time. When Machuky talked or 'jived' to the crowd, everybody would respond, likening the whole happening to the traditional rural musical fiestas where the singing is based on the call-and-response pattern. In the dance-hall setting the deejay gradually replaced the traditional soloist, who normally leads the singing by rehearsing the lines of the songs as they are sung. The singers or 'choir' repeat the lead soloist's words in harmony and rhythm, making sure that their response is well timed and the melody right. It is as if the people must have in their possession a leading inspiration, a personal co-ordinator, conductor of their musical events. However, it is fair to say that the modern deejay is much more than that. He is a translator, an originator and a star performer because he is an accepted music-maker.

But since Machuky the deejay business has developed enormously. He was superseded on the Coxsone sound by King

Stitch, 'the Ugly One'. King Stitch did far more talking than Machuky. He, Stitch, was more boisterous, forceful and down-to-earth or 'rootsy'. Stitch would use rhymes like these: 'This sound is the best by any test. I am the ugly one, I'll meet you at sundown. Be prepared to draw.' That is stuff from the cinemas. Deejays love going to cinemas because they draw inspiration from films. 'This sound leads the way every day, come what may.' Or, 'Move and groove and get in the mood. Let the music rock you.' The deejays would exhort the girls to grab a partner and 'Rub dis yah tune yah.' 'Hold on to the one you love the best, cause it's sure gonna be your musical test.' 'Hold on tight and feel all right in the middle of the night.' These phrases and rhymes were of a jocular and social type, which was meant to be light-hearted as opposed to soul-searching and conscience-stirring. The latter type of deejaying had to wait until the early 1970s and the arrival of Big Youth.

Before we discuss Big Youth, though, it is necessary to bring in U-Roy, the 'daddy' (as the deejays admit) of them all. U-Roy came into prominence as number one deejay for King Tubby's Home Town Hi-Fi. He is strictly an originator and the acknowledged teacher of all deejays. The fierce competition of the sound-system business meant that a would-be deejay had to possess some potential to reach to the top or hold his own among the acknowledged greats. U-Roy was not just good but exceptional. He possessed an abundance of musical talent. Between 1966 and 1972 the scene was dominated by U-Roy. King Tubby's sound at the time played a good deal of Treasure Isle music. This label was owned by Duke Reid of sound-system fame in an earlier epoch. The music was called 'rock steady' because it was slower than the 'ska' which it had succeeded. The rock-steady rhythm consisted of a continuously steady bass line, which is reminiscent of the rumba box bass line of the by then outdated mento/calypso music. This style of music fitted the mood of the Jamaican lovers of popular folk music. Dance-hall patrons found the music ideal for close dancing.

U-Roy caught the mood and was ready to lead the way.

King Tubby himself was a pioneer in the reggae music field. He was the first sound-system operator or owner to use 'versions' of standard discs on his sound system. Thus, all the great and favourite Treasure Isle hits were versioned with U-Roy mixing it with the singing. (Versioned means that when a record is made the A side carries the voices and lyrics with a balanced mix of the instruments and sounds. The B side is a repeat of the A side's rhythm but with an altered dub-mix that gives the deejay time and space to do his thing.) Tunes by the Techniques, Alton Ellis, the Paragons and the Cables were dubbed or versioned, and when the deejays talked over the versions it was as if one was hearing a different tune, although one knew the tune. The dub versions opened a new gate into the domain of music. The less privileged in Jamaican society were not slow to see the opening and how to make their way through the gates. U-Roy came to Duke Reid's attention when the Duke heard versions of his productions (because by then Duke Reid was a music producer) on King Tubby's sound. The Duke saw that the dance crowd loved it wherever the sound was played. Thus U-Roy got his chance with the Treasure Isle label.

The poetry of the deejays' lyrics held as much attraction as the content of the lyrics or the rhythm of the 'rapping' or talking style. One of the dance-hall ravers' favourites was U-Roy's hit cover version of 'My Girl,' which goes like this:

> Now this is a musical lesson, When I am through with you I know you will be missing.
> Good gosh, yeah, tell it to yuh.
> Well, the first ting yuh should learn to do is your owna ting, I tell yuh.
> As I am going to give yuh a whipping, as I wouda tell yuh, baby.
> And yuh will get a whipping, get a whipping, get a whipping, as I woulda tell yuh.
> Hey, let the music rock yuh.
> So I gonna whip yuh wid de rod of correction ...

Or 'Way Down South':

Way down south where the little children used to play, you
could hear the good brother would say,
   So you gotta be careful of the little things you do, as I
would tell you.
   Baby, you got to let some go and let some stay, as I would
tell you.
   You gotta let love shine bright each and every day, as I
would tell you.
   Yeah, baby, gotta come on down and let mi si yuh do your
ting.
   And let mi si yuh swing, I tell you, come on and work yuh
show....

U-Roy had the ability to reach a cross-section of the Jamaican
population, and all the lovers of the local popular music
loved U-Roy. But not only in Jamaica. Not long after U-Roy
distinguished himself in the Jamaican musical scene, he
became well known in the UK and a firm favourite of the
Afro-Caribbean population of that country. He was the chief
inspiration for potential and actual black deejays on the UK
sound-system circuit.

By 1972–3 a deejay by the name of Big Youth had fully
established himself in Jamaica. He worked a sound system
called Tippa-Tone, which was very popular in Kingston and
all over the country; it drew very large crowds. Big Youth
had to be different from U-Roy. He was more of a rebel
figure, a symbol of everything that the 'rude boy' stood for.
The name Big Youth is reminiscent of 'Big Boy', who in
Jamaican folklore is the antithesis of childhood order and the
authority of guardianhood. The socio-cultural rebellion that
took place in the late 1960s in Jamaica was a general and
higher manifestation of the 'Big Boy' syndrome. Equally, the
term 'rude boy' is nothing more than a generalized form of
the individualized 'Big Boy'. The 'rude boys', or the rebellious
element of the Kingston ghettos, easily and readily identified
with Big Youth. He spoke their language, lyrically and rhythmically. On vinyl records Big Youth was an instant hit. His
'S90 Skank', produced by the late Keith Hudson, stamped Big
Youth as a real challenger of U-Roy for deejay supremacy.

The S90 was a popular motorcycle: 'If you ride like light-ning, you crash like tundah!' That is the opening line of the tune. Motorbikes crash their riders frequently, so Big Youth was expounding the fears, caution and expectations of bike riders. Big Youth's style was slow and deliberate, although by 1974 he speeded up his rapping, something which U-Roy was already doing in order to avoid imitators. It is quite strange that a great proportion of UK reggae lovers think that Smiley Culture, Pappa Levi and the rest are originators of fast talking. They are not. U-Roy was talking at the greatest possible speed back in the early 1970s in order to escape imitators like Dennis Alcapone, Scotty and less successful aspirants. Big Youth eventually blossomed into a very good singer and sang hit records – once the beat of the music had changed, which happens frequently in reggae music. Big Youth was the first to master the new style. A change in the music necessitates changes in dance movements, singing and deejaying styles and even lyrical content.

Big Youth widened the field of deejaying by drawing hea-vily on ghetto experiences, phrases, terms and styles in order to express ghetto life. Big Youth was the first deejay to dispense with vocal harmony on the cover version. Up to his time deejays would rely heavily on the vocal harmony dubbed into the cover version so as to make sure that the record-buying public did not forget the original vocal release, which would invariable be a popular hit. That way financial success was guaranteed. But Big Youth chose to rely on his abilities, so he filled out the newly acquired space himself, thereby introducing to the record-buying public the deejay in his own right. More freedom for the deejay meant more creativity and invention, which in turn stimulated the interest of a record-buying public relatively starved of socio-cultural power, control and authority. It had the potential (other things being equal) to establish means whereby a people could have proper images of their worth and value that could then be reflected in relationships that were respected, as opposed to worthless stereotyping and constantly damaged relationships.

Reggae Deejaying in the UK

There can be no doubt that reggae music has opened an enormous door for a great many black youths to be creative, inventive and successful, even if only on a material level. At the same time, a number of seasoned entrepreneurs have done well from their own investments and efforts. Like it or not (many people do *not* like it), reggae music is a challenge. In a sense, one could quite easily say that the challenge which was thrown down in Jamaica was eagerly taken up in the UK. The Afro-Caribbean people who became the UK's black immigrants settled in the country, from the early 1950s, with their language, cultural habits and customs. As far as culture is concerned, however, the Jamaican portion of the Afro-Caribbean settler communities up and down the UK have exhibited a conspicuous tendency to be culturally different, precisely because they possess a strong cultural heritage. This fact was once ignored and pretended away, but over time the truth has revealed itself, and now most serious students of cultural matters have acknowledged that Jamaicans have a valid and vibrant culture, which is rich in content, very meaningful and relevant in a wider world socio-cultural context.

Today in the UK the fruits of the labours and efforts of the first-generation Afro-Caribbean immigrants are reaped by their descendants, the second- and third-generation 'Afro-British', if you like (some would say Black British or British Black). In terms of language and music the black youths of Britain are well endowed. Most of them know Afro-Lingua. Even if they do not speak it regularly, they understand when it is spoken to them because they have been brought up on it. Few people realize that most of the first-generation immigrants speak their native dialects, with distinct accents, styles and rhythms. Immigrants especially from Dominica and St Lucia (to a much lesser extent Grenada, Trinidad and St Vincent) speak a French Creole language, which is a mixture of French and African languages (and, to a lesser degree, Spanish and English). Of the strictly English-speaking islands and territories Jamaica has, in my view, the most highly developed Creole or Patois. It is sufficiently not English and not understood by an average English person for translation to be necessary. The Jamaican Patois – I call it Afro-Lingua – is not English spoken in a local accent; it is another language which is fighting for credibility.

The advent of the Rastafari people and their overt application of spirit and effort in cultural matters have served to broaden the frontiers of cultural discoveries, inventions and achievements. The black youths of Britain are black not only in terms of biology and colour of skin but also in terms of culture. There is a large amount of cultural confusion, and this is reflected quite often in behaviour. However, cultural confusion should not be mistaken for the absence of a valid cultural formation with a rich cultural content. The young blacks of Britain are aware of the cultural position that confronts them. They know that they are in a culturally fluid situation; they are free, therefore, to chop and change, to adopt this or that lifestyle, and this is done more often than not. Still, young British black people know exactly what is going on, and a substantial number of them are prepared to live a double cultural life in the sense that one minute they are 'Cockney' or 'Brummie' and the next minute they are 'ranking ghettoites', 'reggae steppers' or Rasta.

Because the Afro-Caribbean culture is an alternative culture it serves to succour those youths who, from time to time, seek an alternative mode of expression that reflects better their own personal transformation with its attendant reformed conception of life. The ghetto is the basis of the alternative culture. Thus on many occasions when the open society fails the youths, it is the ghetto that rescues them. The sound system and dance circuit are very important to the Afro-Caribbean people. For those of the ghetto they are the ultimate in social expression, or so it appears. The employed and unemployed look forward to going to parties, 'blues dances' and 'ravings'. Everybody dresses up to the best of his or her ability, money at the ready (even the unemployed find money at these times), and enters into the parties; everyone

socializes in a culturally distinct style which indicates immediately that one is at an Afro-Caribbean party. The party or
blues dance is like a sports club, a free meeting, a market
place, a factory, without membership or directors and
managers or stalls and so forth. The alternative language in
this situation is the only medium of verbal expression.

It is at the blues dances that one gets to hear the latest
linguistic inventions. The deejays come into their own at
blues dances because those are where they make their names
and obtain their seal of approval and acceptance. At the blues
dance people would say to one another: 'Ahrite, wha' apen
man (sah), lang time mi no si yuh.' 'Ah bwoy a so yi goh, mi
jus a cruise.' 'Well, ahrite den, cool noh.'

For a long time reggae deejays in the UK would just imitate
their Jamaican favourites and mentors. This practice persisted for a variety of reasons through the 1960s and 1970s
until around 1983–4, when deejays from the third generation
of immigrant settlers started working sound systems. These
youths, though, were the beneficiaries of a well established
tradition. Youth deejays like Smiley Culture, Pappa Levi,
Asher Senator and many more exhibit well, in my view, the
real meaning for the black youths in Britain, who are ambitious, creative, positive and willing to achieve. These black
youths have extended cultural strongholds that are normally
well fortified.

Fast-rapping is the name of their style. But what is interesting about these young deejays is that they are trying hard and
successfully to reach a white audience too. Over the past
seven years or so a substantial number of white people have
been buying reggae music and supporting reggae concerts.
The lyrics of reggae music are strictly Afro-Lingua; therefore
there is a problem for the whites in terms of understanding.
Smiley Culture's contribution to culture and reggae is that he
was quick to see the problem of understanding the lyrics. His
first record, 'Cockney Translation', sought to translate for
the white record-buying public the meanings of certain key
phrases. This is how Smiley Culture puts it across in 'Cockney Translation':

Cockney is not a language – it's only a slang which was originated in East London.

It was respected for the style and different pronunciation, but wasn't used by any and any man ...

Cockneys have names like Arthur and Tell Boy. We have names like Winston, Lloyd and Leroy.

Cockney say 'jam', we live ina 'yard',
Cockney say 'shooter', we 'bus gun',
Cockney say 'terrific', we say 'gwaan',
Cockney say 'ole bill', we say 'dotty Babylon' ...

But Smiley Culture knows that he is a talented originator. His release 'Police Officer' is appealing to the white Cockney police to go easy on him. At the same time he is telling his listeners a story about his dealings with some police who stopped him in Victoria, on his way from East London, where he had been visiting his mother. This record became a massive hit for Smiley Culture. About the same time that Smiley Culture was releasing 'Cockney Translation' Pappa Levi released a tune called 'Mi God, Mi King'. This record contained no cockney slang, but it is an epoch-making record which brought Levi a great deal of fame and some fortune. This record is noted for its introduction to reggae of the fast-talking style. In reggae there is always room for innovation (in this respect reggae is more like jazz than any other popular music with an ethnic connection), and this is an important aspect of the tradition of the music. It is not difficult to see why reggae is characterized by change. In reggae competition plays as great a role as culture. For the artists, or for a good many of them, the need to be different, appealing and successful is uppermost in their thoughts. For the reggae fans, or most of them, what is most appreciated in artists is their originality, professionalism and ability to deliver good and meaningful lyrics in relation to life experiences (like rhythm and blues) and cultural mores. In this respect Pappa Levi is an innovator.

In my view, reggae music, and especially the deejaying

aspect of the music, has established itself, without any doubt at all, as the principal transmitter of the Jamaican language (Afro-Lingua). A substantial proportion of young black people in Britain are keen to speak the language because by doing so they realize that they are breaking down self-alienation. Living in a society which constantly reminds them that they are different, the black youths who turn to their own cultural roots for identity find solace in speaking Afro-Lingua. The fact that both the Rastafarian Movement and reggae music have promoted a great interest in the nature and meaning of the Jamaican language reinforces the eagerness of black youth to speak the language. There is another compelling side to the Afro-Lingua: it is serving to maintain interest in the language, and this is a more recent development.

Lately we have witnessed the rise of poetic literature in Afro-Lingua. Poets like Louise Bennett, Michael Smith (who has passed away), Mutabaruka, Jean Breeze, Linton Kwesi Johnson and others are busy tearing down the barriers that divide people on the linguistic level of life. It must be said, however, that Louise Bennett is a very old hand at writing poetry in Jamaican Patois. But the rise of what is termed 'dub poetry' has secured for Ms Bennett recognition as a major pioneer of written Patois. Patois dub poetry is now studied in quite a few schools, especially in the Inner London Education Authority-controlled schools of London. If a language is to prosper and flourish, especially in its formative years, it needs transmitting agencies like music and literature, and these, I am happy to say, are available to Afro-Lingua.

Afro-Lingua is a very rich, informal language. It is in a state of constant development. Its informality makes it very flexible, and this, in turn, encourages all sorts of invention and verbal permutation. Consequently, the wealth of possibilities that are revealed serve to motivate great interest in Afro-Lingua. The black youths in Britain who speak the Jamaican Patois do so for the same reasons as the black youths in Jamaica do. They speak it in order to obtain a sense of security, to harbour a feeling of togetherness and as a symbol of attachment to their cultural roots. Politically, these youths desire a greater measure of socio-cultural freedom. By speaking Afro-Lingua they are only asserting their intention to realize that freedom as they mature into adulthood. For them it is now or never!

5

The Literature of the Black Experience

JAMES BERRY

James Berry outlines a journey that started with the traumatic Middle Passage, continued through freedom, through political independence, and is carried forward in Britain now. Black writers struggle to express and explore their people's need to rid themselves of definitions thrust on them by others and to redefine what they are, what they are about. They are helped by the Rastas and the oral poetry discussed in previous chapters. Indeed, these merge in writer-performers like Linton Kwesi Johnson. What began as the 'unravelling of a restricted existence' – masterfully achieved, for instance, by V. S. Naipaul – is becoming a quest for an expansion of spirit in order to articulate both the outrage and the exhilaration of the black experience.

The Freedom Obsession

The confiscation of freedom made a terrific impact on Afro-Caribbean people. The forced-labour experience they endured – that not belonging to yourself, that endless no-pay work, that being ineligible for common rights that uphold human dignity, that way of life called slavery – translated itself into a burdensome loss. Freedom became a haunting thought and prayer and dream of Afro-Caribbean people. It aroused resistance. It has come to arouse a dynamic desire for reclamation.

From early on, finding themselves landed in the Caribbean,

the Africans held on to the belief that they would get back to their African 'nations', to welcomes and rejoicings. That hope stayed with them year after year and decade after decade. On plantations on every island the people revolted regularly; each rebellion ended more bloodily and was more brutally crushed than the last. The freedom longing continued, revived in each new century and came to be poured out in Caribbean writing.

In the literature there is a culture-crossing fraught with pressures, injustice, non-sharing. Unable to adapt to the culture values and systems of the new way of life that adopted them or to share meaningfully in it, the people in turn eventually rejected it. They searched for and dusted off their own culture-style models and traditions and set about updating them. There is now an obsession to cleanse the psyche of the experience of being drawn upon purely as a resource – as horsepower, or land, or gold, or North Sea oil. So while there is outrage and anguish and struggle, there is also celebration.

Naturally, language has been given a new and central role. It is clear that plantation life did not completely destroy the African-ness of the people. Overlord's language was not swallowed whole. Though the African was forced to speak English on the plantation, by being chained at work to another who spoke a different native tongue, his background response to language was kept alive. His descendants inherited a new language. We see that while Creole, or 'nation language', has retained a general foundation of English words, the sounds, grammar and rhythms are West African-based. Not, then, 'dialect interference in English', Caribbean 'nation' speech is simply a different language, which struggles to find appropriate adjustments in order to settle down as the mother tongue into which it has grown. Given that background, it should not be a surprise that the novel *New Day*, written in the 1940s by Jamaican V. S. Reid, should have come to prominence immediately, attracted intense critical attention and acclaim and gained a place of honour among Caribbean novels. Both the language used and the event that prompted it helped to underline the importance of *New Day*.

The first really meaningful official move towards national self-rule in Jamaica inspired it. And the novel has a people's voice. It has as its setting a particularly bloody bid for freedom – the Morant Bay Rebellion of 1865. It uses and celebrates the Jamaican people's yearning and struggle. The writer centres his work on the historic rebellion that caused the death of eighteen white people on the side of the Crown and planters; among the people the militia and court trials accounted for hundreds of deaths, hundreds of floggings and thousands of cottages destroyed. The New Constitution of 1944 brought near self-government and full adult suffrage. Though slavery had been abolished in 1838, the people still could not vote freely. The island's ruling class had long since found effective ways to limit the kinds and numbers of people who could vote. *New Day* reconstructs the bitter time of 1865, linking historical struggle with new-found national status.

New Day Tells its Story

An ageing middle-class man narrates the story. Overwhelmed by his history and his thoughts, he looks back on the rebellion:

> I am restless tonight. Through the half-opened window near where I sit, night winds come down the Blue Mountains to me. Many scents come down on the wind ... even wounds from musket balls.

> Are you a-hear, George William Gordon? And Paul Bogle ... All o' you Dead Hundreds ...?'

> There is a list of names posted to the court-house at Morant Bay. It is headed: *Executed Rebels* ... Rebels? ... what is wrong with men calling you a rebel?

> Bide awhile, Lucille ... Davie has seen more than any of us ...

> Tongues o' flames crackle at mangrove wood ... Will they hear me? A man who marched with Bogle?

Deacon Bogle and the Stoney Gut men fought for freedom,
but they ha' got the chains hammered on tighter instead ...

Memories of the hurt of events seek a reconciliation, and
words revel in a peaceful victory: 'O – how our people are a-
sing ... like deep-running water ... from their throats to greet
this new day.'

The language of *New Day* is prayerful, filled with impas-
sioned cleansing. Yet, strictly, it does not reflect accurately
the idiom of the Jamaican masses (as will be shown later).
New Day language created a fusion of 'people's' language
and middle-class speech, which, with its closer and more
sustained contacts with standard English, it absorbed. The
work points to all sorts of intentions to transcend, link and
unite levels and classes of Jamaican society. In the end its
philosophy may not be robust enough to satisfy reality. Yet
what works at all works well. Strong textures of nature and
landscape and the people's way of life are interwoven excel-
lently. Characters emerge from a particular landscape. 'Day-
cloud' peeps through with its special quality. 'Sea-breeze' has
its own 'anger-marks'. 'Arrows wave' above a cane-field and
say, 'The juice is ripe'. Sensations of eating mangoes, bammie
cakes and molasses are delights as sweet as the voices of the
kling-kling bird.

Since other Caribbean writers have gone on to use 'nation
language' extensively in their writing, *New Day* may well
have helped to challenge strongly the bluffs of standard
English, with its insistence on singular validity.

Restricted Existence

Pointing to a restricted existence that meets continued resistance in Guyana in 1957, A. J. Seymour's poem 'First of
August' tells of

Over a hundred years of a people
Toiling against climate
Working against prejudice
Growing within an alien framework

Cramped, but stretching its limbs ...

Then a reply comes from Jamaica, from poet/novelist/playwright/painter Roger Mais, who as a severe critic of colonial policy was jailed for publishing writing considered to be seditious. His poem 'Men of Ideas' echoes:

A hundred years is not too long
For the seed to burst its husk under the ground
And cleave a path and press upward
And thrust a green blade in triumph at the sun.
Do not be anxious for the house that is a-building,
For the unsown acres under the plough,
For all things await a time and a season ...

Traditional Great-House Indifference

The post-slavery Caribbean inherited both an upper- and a middle-class traditional scorn and indifference towards the general deprivation of the masses. Although the people's villages grew up around former slave estates, the Great Houses manifested neither a social conscience nor an involvement with the well-being and development of their former unpaid workers. Divisions could only widen.

In his book *Christopher* Geoffrey Drayton writes about a white teenage boy's relationship with his frustrated sugar-planter father. The boy wants to understand the lives of black people around him. He feels caged living in an isolated Great House. He has no companions. The father's manner is intended to show how civilized he is. In fact, his actions make him formal and repressive. As his son's energies are unused, his thoughts and inner feelings intense, he wanders about. He climbs the roof of the house. Ready to come down, he finds the ladder that he used has been removed and that a servant has been sent to summon him to his father. 'You must be careful next time not to walk in the gutters,' the father says.

The boy rages, 'Was it you who had the ladder taken away then?'

His father's grim laugh tells him he has guessed correctly.

The Tension of Poverty and Wealth –
or is it Poverty and Poverty?

In contrast to *Christopher*, Roger Mais's books are usually about social deprivation and coping with uncheckable impulses in such a condition. His broodings usually find voice in shack settings with characters who may well deliver news like, 'Mis' Brody's clubfoot bwoy get run over.' Here in a short story, 'Blackout', he highlights racial tension with its ready, compulsive fear, its links with a sense of superiority and sheer poverty and humiliation.

Set in a black-out in wartime Kingston, Jamaica, the story is about a young white American woman and a black Jamaican. The brief meeting takes place at a poorly lit bus stop.

The tall, slightly stooping figure arrives and unnerves the waiting passenger: 'the thing that struck her immediately was the fact that he was black.' He confronts her and asks her for a light for his saved-up cigarette stub. Though she is smoking, she has no matches or lighter and tells the man that. He has simply expected a light from her lighted cigarette. Realizing the intention in his request, she watches him with a new and cautious hesitation. 'There was a suggestion of intimacy about such an act'; there was 'pride and challenge in his look'; his 'steady gaze never left her face'. She sees 'a curious look of hunger and unrest about his eyes'. She holds her hand out, intending him to take the cigarette. He bends over her hand, lights his stubbed cigarette, straightens up and inhales with satisfaction. Then, he notices, she does not put the cigarette back between her lips. She flicks it away.

'I'm sorry I made you waste a whole cigarette,' he says. 'Plenty more where that came from, eh? ... Good thing you're a woman ... I'd give you something to think about.'

She thinks, 'In America they lynch them for less than this.'

He says, 'This isn't America ...'

The bus comes. His eyes are fixed on her. She does not look back as she boards it: 'just as well that she did not see him bend forward with that swift hungry movement, retrieving from the gutter the half-smoked cigarette she had thrown away'.

Restless for Change

Barbadian George Lamming brought out in 1953 his *In the Castle of My Skin*, a novel alive with a special restlessness for change. Set in the 1930s and 1940s, the book accumulates its impact indirectly.

The story takes place in a Barbadian village and is filled with the apparently inconsequential activities of childhood. Particularly, though, there are Ma and Pa. But the boys explore and unravel a restricted existence. They speculate with little-formed ideas and misunderstood information.

G's mother gives him a bath in the open yard, and boys peep at him from behind the neighbour's fence. Bob, in fact, has climbed on to the swaying fence and his mother speaks: 'You kill the neighbour pumpkin vine, and on the back of it you laugh?' Bob looks at the vine. His mother shouts, 'Well, what you going to tell her?'

The boys roam hauntedly. They go to the seaside. Their laughter lost in the washing of the sea waves, they watch crabs creep up the slope of sand in single file. The waves come up and the crabs wait, crouching for the water to pass over them. The boys romp and lark about. They philosophize.

'What ever happen?' Trumper asked.

'The way a thing put itself together,' Boy Blue said. 'You hear something, an' it come to you as a kind of surprise, then it connect up with another something you'd hear long time back, an' what with one thing an' another, they all put themselves together into a big something. Suddenly when they all together you see yourself face to face with something that is true or very very strange. Or it make you remember something that you didn't remember all the time.'

Disguised self-contempt has a way of expressing an unconscious worry. It has interesting ways of surfacing; it may be
expressed as veiled confusion, as hearty bantering, as light or
serious abuse or merely as statements left unchallenged.

Trumper, it is said, has a record. At nine years old he
committed a crime. Too young to go to prison, he was sent to
a reformatory school. Among other punishments there, his
eyebrows were shaved off. Trumper does not confirm or deny
the story. Anyway, everybody can see his eyebrows are still
queer. The saving grace of Trumper's face is the colour of his
skin. He has the kind of skin that is called 'fair skin, or light
skin, or, best of all, clear skin'.

The book's narrator goes on to explain:

> Neither of us could be called crystal. And there weren't many
> in the village who weren't black. Simply black. But though we
> were nearly all black, we all used the colour as a weapon
> against interference. If we lost our temper we would charge
> the other with being a black fool, or a black ass. Among the
> better educated, and the Great, the obscenities might not have
> been used in public, but they were affected in the same way.
> They often said of the village teacher how very bright he was,
> but he was so black ... Sometimes we amused ourselves by
> asking each other why he was so black. And someone would
> say it wasn't good for the brain. And there was always the
> danger of the blood getting black ...
>
> Boy Blue was still looking up at the sky, testing the strength
> of his eye by the light of the sun ...

Quietly intense, with a poetic tone, the language of the book
impresses generally with a classical mood that works in a
Caribbean context.

The white landlord obsesses. Living on a hill overlooking
the village, the landlord exercises control through a black
overseer. An unease, an untouchable menace, entraps and
engages Ma and Pa powerfully.

> [Ma:] I don't care who want land or who take land, the
> nations or anybody else, I'd only like to ask all o' them put
> together what they goin' do with it ...

[Pa:] I get so frighten sometimes when I ask myself what next, an' I ain't see no answer comin' to help. Sometimes the feelin' want to stay with you like 'tis a sickness, an' you get away by pretending you doin' something else. You try to talk 'bout this than an' the next, an' if you young you go out an' drink ...

The Beguiling Maze

Trinidadian V. S. Naipaul published *Miguel Street* in 1959. In this group of short stories, arranged as a short novel, desire for freedom shows itself differently.

Set in a slum area of Port-of-Spain, Trinidad, the characters are people frenzied with activity yet unaware that they are totally lost. Unable to grasp the fact that their activities will change nothing, unable to understand that they have no real ways and means to make progress towards what their needs and ambitions call for, the people are hopeless imitators. They have names like Bogart and Wordsworth, Big Foot and Hat. Though trapped in total ignorance and poverty, the people want to show themselves as big.

The stories are unravelled through the eyes of a boy. Yet we soon see that the details are selected with meticulous care. Scenes, anecdotes and colourful, outlandish behaviour come together with artistry. Even laughter is treachery and self-mockery. Thought and activity construct a vivid nightmare, and the creators have no idea that it is all their own creation. Comic failures, the characters are a joke.

Big Foot is 'really big and really black'. Big Foot is 'sulky' and fearsome, like one of those 'terrible dogs' that never bark. The inside walls of George's partly broken-down wooden house are 'grey and black with age'. He paints the outside pink. The film *Casablanca* is an influence: young men adopt the hard-boiled attitudes of Bogart. A man takes the film actor's name.

Then Bogart pretends that he makes his living by tailoring. He even offers money and has a 'Tailor and Cutter' sign put up. But nobody remembers Bogart making any clothes. Similarly, next door the carpenter Popo, with the big 'Builder and

Carpenter' sign, planes and chisels all day, yet makes nothing. When asked what he is making, his answer always is: 'Ha, boy! That's the question. I making the thing without a name.' Pressed to make an egg-stand, Popo asks the customer, 'Who you making it for?' The customer says, 'Ma.' Popo laughs, saying, 'Think she going use it?' Popo never manages to earn any money. His wife earns the money. Popo says, 'Man not make for work.' Yet Hat says, 'Popo is a man-woman. Not a proper man.'

The activities are a strong mix of violence, lies and petty crimes. Hat and friends use Bogart's room as a club-house. Involved with the police over cock-fighting and gambling, Bogart uses bribery to clear himself. One day Bogart says, 'Ha! I mad to break old George tail up, you hear.'

The value of masculinity lies in winning respect by expressing oneself as an excellent beater of woman and children. The women are not 'proper' women. They earn the money, do the house- and yard-work and take beatings from their men. George's wife dies. It is agreed that 'The woman dead from blows'. George fills himself with rum and goes crying in the streets. He beats his chest, asking everybody to forgive him. Somebody says it's 'all God work'. Somebody else, looking worried, says, 'A girl making baby for me.' Hat tells him not to be stupid. 'It have some woman making a living this way, you know.'

To have a special skill is to be a pavement sweeper. To be an aristocrat is to be a cart-driver. Though Man-Man does not have a job, he is never idle. The written word hypnotizes Man-Man. He will use up a whole day writing one word. Man-Man puts himself up as a candidate in elections and gets three votes. Man-Man sees God. Man-Man gets to the stage when he knows he has a messianic mission and wants to undergo a crucifixion. He gets himself tied to a cross and shouts, 'Stone me, brethren.' A big stone hits Man-Man. He bawls, 'Cut this stupidness out ... you hear?'

A boy runs up the steps of his house and calls, 'Ma. It have a man outside.' The man has said he wants to watch bees. Ma tells the boy to stay there with him. Both squat under a palm tree and watch the bees. The man stands up and says he is a poet. Impressed, the boy asks his name. 'B. Wordsworth,' he says. 'Black Wordsworth ...'

If these stories did not suffer from an absence of compassion and a redemptive human outlet, surely they would be masterpieces.

It is also worth noting that, concerned with the art of winning the widest readership, Naipaul uses standard English words, yet through the construction of his dialogue and particular sounds he captures Caribbean speech. You will notice 'The woman dead from blows', not 'De ooman ded fram blows' or 'Ded fram blow dem'.

Travellers in Reflection and Hope

Somewhere between the 1950s and 1960s a group of Caribbean writers came to Britain and became exiled here, fulfilling themselves with their most impressive and important novel-writing. All of them – V. S. Naipaul, George Lamming, Samuel Selvon, E. R. Braithwaite, Wilson Harris, Michael Anthony, Andrew Salkey, Edgar Mittelholzer – would have found a minute readership in the Caribbean at the time. Also, they would have discovered London to be a much more stimulating and creative base from which to write. Yet their enforced exile fades into insignificance when compared with the important Caribbean continuity they established through their writing. All the same, it should be noted that the new black people, born in Britain, have a different stance and emphasis. But before we turn to how the cultural focus has changed, we should look briefly at the work of a few of those 1950s writers.

In *The Emigrants* (1954) George Lamming's people are on a ship to England. They speculate about themselves as travellers to real freedom. And being there on the ship, in the near reality of the new life, is in itself a heightening and strange acquisition.

A Trinidadian says, 'Trinidad ain't no place for a man to live; an' that's why you see I clearin' out ... not'ing too bad can happen that ain't happen before ...'

A Barbadian says, ' ... only las' week the papers say how three or four men run off from Barbados in a yacht. The owners couldn't understan' what happen next mornin' ... It happen every day in Trinidad.'

A Jamaican says, 'Me see worst in Jamaica ... men get on as if stowaway had more right to de ship than those who pay passage. Them put up gangway themself ...'

A Grenadian says it isn't where a man goes that matters most, "tis what he do after ...'

Somebody says, 'This blasted world is a hell of a place. Why the hell a man got to leave where he born when he ain't thief not'in', nor kill nobody ...'

Somebody else says, 'Ah goin' to a school in Liverpool ...'

A reply comes, 'You's the only man on dis ship who sort o' know for certain what he doin' ...'

And it has all happened like a 'sudden big push from the back ... when you weren't looking'.

Caribbean people had taken the initiative: to move, to travel, not to await approval, to settle at the centre of their world. Jamaican folklorist and poet Louise Bennett celebrated the historical change with 'Colonization in Reverse':

> ... Wat a devilment a Englan!
> Dem face war an brave de worse,
> But I'm wonderin' how dem gwine stan'
> Colonizin' in reverse.

The New Days in Britain

As contributors to Caribbean writing in Britain, writers like Andrew Salkey and Wilson Harris and others have exposed the experience and voices of Afro-Caribbean people. Yet, with its certain roots-level vigour, Trinidadian Samuel Selvon's writings struck his readers immediately with their vital freshness. His stories about the new Caribbean people in

Britain in the 1950s and 1960s enjoyed a special popularity. Existing mostly in insecurity, poised between finding a job and a home, between passionate encounters with women and loneliness, between homesickness and wild gaiety, between sober moments and times of mad, impulsive acts, the people in his writings insisted on survival with some laughs.

In Selvon's novel *The Lonely Londoners* (1956) Moses has a 'soft heart'. Acknowledging the obligation and automatic duty of someone known in the Caribbean, he welcomes all sorts of cousins, and friends of cousins, and friends of friends new from 'back home', who arrive 'straight to his room in the Water [Bayswater]', bearing his name. Number one London contact man, Moses is welfare worker, liaison officer, housing minister.

Moses cries out, 'Jesus Christ, I never see thing so. I don't know these people at all ... I catching my arse as it is, how I could help them out?' When Moses asks who gave his name as contact, he is told it was Jackson. 'Jackson is a bitch,' Moses says. 'He know that I seeing hell myself.'

In spite of the protests Moses finds himself sitting on a bench smoking a 'Woods' (Woodbine cigarette) at Waterloo Station, waiting for the boat-train. Waiting too, a fellow West Indian asks Moses if he knows where he can find a 'bigger place'. Moses says, 'Big City was telling me yesterday it have a house down by the Grove (Ladbroke Grove) what have some vacant rooms.'

A whole lot of people come to meet arrivals; 'big oldtalk' goes on. Moses notices a Jamaican 'test' (smart fellow) 'hustling tenants'. But Moses does not consider himself any saint either. He is Trinidadian. Since everyone in England believes every black face is Jamaican, Moses is not a man to spoil anything. He assists an English reporter who wants to know why so many people are leaving Jamaica. Was the recent hurricane so devastating? 'Yes,' Moses says. 'Plenty people get kill ... I was sitting down in my house and suddenly ... hurricane blow the roof off.'

For a while the British literary scene accepted the amusement of Selvon's writing as the only genuine voice and all that the exotic calypsonians had to say. But then another writer appeared.

E. R. Braithwaite from Guyana published his novel *To Sir With Love* in 1959 and took us into his experiences of racism. The main character is a black teacher who works in a tough London school. Smarting from painful race discrimination throughout months of job-hunting, the teacher now has pupils who are products of inner-city decay.

A pupil's mother dies. The mother has been well known and popular locally. The pupil's classmates decide to collect money among themselves and buy flowers for his mother's funeral. Then the teacher realizes that, in the absence of the bereaved pupil, no classmate is willing to be the bearer of flowers. It dawns on him that though the pupil's mother was white, his father is West Indian. Though again feeling himself attacked racially, he has to ask the pupils to explain why the flowers are suddenly causing concern. Moira stands up. 'We can't take them, Sir,' she says. Asked why not, she answers, 'It's what people would say if they saw us going to a coloured person's home.'

Renewal, Outcry, Resistance, Memory, Outrage

With political independence in the 1960s, Afro-Caribbean people soon found themselves in a desperate state. A reckoning came home to them. After the dehumanizing experience of slavery and the restrictions and deprivations of colonial life, they had a need to redefine themselves. The people who were supposed to have been lords and masters were suddenly seen as essentially able to view black people only as a resource, like mules or coal or gold mines. In the process, what had happened to them, the used?

In Britain, and simultaneously in the Caribbean, writers, artists, activists, community workers found themselves obsessed with ideas and actions that could be readily described as designed to cleanse the psyche, the emotions, the memory, of domination and contempt; to redefine who the

Afro-Caribbean person really is; and to restore a wholesome Africanness to both personality and culture.

A rush of energy began to overwhelm new writers. Not seeking approval, often without an academic or literary background, they had only to sit and write to find that their work was regarded as part of a tradition called 'political' or 'protest literature', like Jamaican Oku Onuora's 'A Slum Dweller Declares', with its outcry:

> wi waan
> fi free
> free from misery ...

The British-based poets are experiencing a similar feeling, though they are responding differently. With subtler and cooler anguish, examining the same condition of deprivation and using the same metaphor of journeying together (though with an all-knowing commentator who only understands about, and believes in, failure), E. A. Markham comments cynically in his 'Inheritance':

> The topless native
> of our ship trusts
> her blue eyes
> for she knows already
> how this trip will end.
> ... My
> predecessors have armed her
> with my secrets.

In his 'Dread Beat and Blood' Linton Kwesi Johnson exposes the wounds:

> ... like fire-claws at my people's peace
> like stones upon a black child's growth
> ... the way cannot be but blood ...

> ... I hurt de pain
> again and again

... O that history should take such a rough route ...

Amryl Johnson asks in 'How Do You Feed the Ghosts?':

How do you feed those emaciated spectres
which rise from the trenches of near
forgotten battles
hungry for recognition?
How do you make the gouged-out mutilations
which cling to the brackish waters of
restless pools
whole again? ...

Offering resistance in his poem 'Coolman', Nkemka Asika
states:

... Coolman
I have some fire
For you coolman ...

In 'Want Fi Goh Rave' Linton Kwesi Johnson is both
outraged by and resistant to deprivation. He implies that
destructive conditions are brought about by lawful thieving
arrangements by which the have-nots are trapped into unlaw-
ful thieving. Sympathy for the victims emerges:

... Ah hear annadah yout-man say
him seh:
mi haffi pick a packit
tek a wallit from a jackit ...

In memory of the women on the slave plantations Grace
Nichols asserts in her marvellous cycle of poems 'I is a Long
Memoried Woman':

... We the women who toil
unadorn
heads tie with cheap
cotton
We the women who cut

clear fetch dig sing
We the women making
something from this
ache-and-pain-a-me
back-o-hardness
Yet we the women
who praises go unsung
who voices go unheard
who deaths they sweep
aside
easy as dead leaves ...

And 'A New Relationship', my own poem, records:

... his silence condemned him
... His task is the undoing of kept retaliations
turned obscenities ...

Black Studies

As long historical contempt had turned into a demand that
they should accept racial disqualification, Caribbean people
had to struggle to revive consciousness of their worth. They
began to reject the state of self-denial into which they had
been forced; they rejected too the assumptions of a Eurocen-
tric history that taught, for example, that Columbus 'discovered' the Caribbean and the Americas, which implied that
the people who lived there had no history of their own.

In response to the intense need to clarify identity and to
reappraise history, black studies were set up in London
around the early 1970s. Sam Morris's course took in the
beginnings of civilization, early religious beliefs, the achievements of ancient Egypt as part of the African continent,
North Africa and the nomads, the ancient kingdoms of
Ghana, Mali and Songhay, Islam's arrival in Africa, contemporary Europe in the eleventh and twelfth centuries, Portuguese exploration of the West African coast, trade between
Europe and Africa, the history of Africa, the Caribbean slave

trade, the value of the trade to Britain, the Caribbean plantation system, the aftermath of slavery, New World black personalities, the Black Power Movement, Pan Africanism and current race relations in Britain. These studies were usually intense experiences. My own poem 'Black Study Students' says something about them:

> Without sacredness of roots there was
> no voice to worship. Little boosting
> of spirit, the deep songs froze.
> ... They became the spectacle of return ...

Reassessment and Africa Reclaimed

In this new phase of reassessment and reclaiming, long-lost Africa became a new-found motherland and Mecca and Eden. Central to the Rastafarians' roots renewal and cultural restoration was always their back-to-Africa idealism. Distinguished poets changed their 'slave' names to African ones. And, associating with the Rastafarian cultural identity, they wore the Rastas' headwear with its distinctive colours.

Then it emerged that Afro-American and Caribbean writers were undergoing a real or imagined African pilgrimage simultaneously. As a slave-descendant returnee to Africa, intensely awakened by the experience, Barbadian Edward Brathwaite wrote his trilogy of poems, 'Rights of Passage', 'Masks' and 'Islands', published together eventually as *The Arrivants*. American Alex Haley brought out his book and the TV serial *Roots* about his return to his African ancestral home. Myself, after some Africa hate poems over the years, I found reconciliation in my imagined return in 'Reclamation':

> ... My sanctuary held no truth
> for I could not enter it.
> ... I knew I must go back
> through groans and griefs
> ... I must absorb you
> Middle Passage

... Here I am.
Here I am, where
at beginning one sun
daubed and brushed me
in silence, and I became
obsessed lover of the dance ...

At the same time this new stimulus aroused greater awareness
of old frustrations or generated new ones. Listen to T-Bone
Wilson in his 'Wild Life':

Is England the gateway?
Every time I think of a new place to live,
It turns out to be
Europe, America, or the
West Indies.
Am I afraid of Africa?

In his 'Discrimination' another London poet, Jawiattika
Blacksheep writes:

IF YOU ARE A TRAMP
NOBODY KNOWS YOU
BUT EVERYBODY SEES YOU
IF YOU ARE A MILLIONAIRE
NOBODY SEES YOU
BUT EVERYBODY KNOWS YOU
IF YOU ARE A RASTAMAN
NOBODY KNOWS YOU
BUT EVERYBODY WANTS
TO CRUCIFY
YOU
ME
US
WE
I AND I ...

In 'A Stray from the Tribe' Rudolph Kizerman tells how the
new black consciousness shakes up a Caribbean would-be
intellectual in Britain:

... The way I remember the cat

is with low cropped hair
and his moustache blocked;
now, he waywardly wears jeans
and digs his share of pot.
Can't see his head
for the hair on top;
for him the really massive Afro is in;
his chicks are not so white any more ...

Along with the look-back-to-Africa drive, nostalgia for the Caribbean recurs too:

I remember back home
Sky blue
Sea clean
Sun warm and radiant.
Looking at himself in the water ...

comes from 'I Remember Back Home' by Donald Peters.

... Me memba how life use to full of fun,
Game galore: chebby, hide-and-find, dog-and-bone,
Mother-and-father, anancy story, riddle.
We no have time fe feel fed up ...

is from Frederick Williams's 'Me Memba Wen'. One or two of my own 'Lucy's Letters' poems could find a place here too.

The Coming of a New and Popular Art Form

Although the arts have commonly been an integral part of social and cultural life on the African continent, the people's traditional skills and crafts disappeared among their descendants during Caribbean slavery. Now, in a new spirit and drive, people whose families for generations had never written a single creative word began to buckle down to the business of expressing themselves through writing. Whether influenced by black studies or not, writers' workshops began to emerge. One of these particularly, the Black Writers' Workshop, keen, intense, committed, developed in Brixton.

In a relaxed atmosphere young men and women often worked on well after midnight, producing work that appeared in booklets published by one of the life-saving small presses of the area, the Black Ink Collective.

Given the new obsession with the written word, it was clear that Bob Marley's reggae music contained the essentials of such a collective voice. While it expressed an absorption of historical and political violence, it was also strikingly mixed with words of his people's folk wisdom and gave voice to a collective knowing uniquely. Black people's experience had cried out for artistic expression. Since independence, shapeless forms wanting moulds had haunted creative black people. To fulfil their artistic needs and to mark their self-discovery new art forms had to be found in their cultural experience and disciplines or to develop from them. Then, through his mass audiences, through the spell his performances weaved, people began to realize that Linton Kwesi Johnson's poetry and performance had absorbed the essentials of Bob Marley's infectious musical art and had individualized them.

Certain obvious qualities made Linton Kwesi Johnson's work particularly popular. Young and fresh, emerging at a crucial historical time, identifying with resistance to racism, showing an up-front commitment to burning social issues, Linton Kwesi and his work became catalysts in the direct expression of outrage against institutionalized injustice and deprivation. Importantly, as shown in previous extracts, its imagery, its guts anguish, its outcry and resistance draw on the deep collective hurt of black people.

'Dub' poetry had come. Not surprisingly, its base was Jamaica, with its reggae roots. Among the popularizers of the form – to be called 'reggae poets', 'people's poets', 'dub poets' – were Linton Kwesi Johnson and Michael Smith. Sadly, the new voice of Michael Smith, with all its extraordinary talent, was soon stilled; he was murdered. His memory lingers, however, and the recordings that testify to his brief spell of intense work remain to influence those who have come after him.

In the work of Linton Kwesi it is the rhythms of speech and sounds of language, together with the style of his performance, that combine to give his work its distinctive Caribbean flavour. In 'It Dread Inna Inglan', for example, his poetry swings from mixed reggae and calypso traditions – the latter highlight an individual or a public event – into a campaign against injustice:

> ... George Lindo
> him noh carry no daggah
> George Lindo
> him is nat no rabbah
> George Lindo
> dem haffi let him go
> George Lindo
> dem bettah free him now!

Linton Kwesi's work reveals a fresh sharpness of mind that expresses itself through the sounds of 'Nation Language': it has an infectious and readily imitated rhythmic structure that accommodates both the presence and the absence of a musical (dub) backing, and it has all the immediacy of the calypso. With these ingredients Linton Kwesi has created a new poetic form that advances the Caribbean folk poetry tradition. It is not surprising that schoolchildren – and adult English poets too – should write and perform poetry in his style. Among young blacks his influence has prompted the mushrooming of new poets.

Two of these new poets stand out particularly: Levi Tafari of Liverpool and Benjamin Zephaniah of London. Both are attractive and popular performers in arts centres, pubs, schools, colleges and theatres. Here is an extract from Tafari's 'Black Roots in Babylon', which won him an Afro-Caribbean Education Resource (ACER) Project Penmanship Award in 1982:

> Spiritually rooted
> Culturally aware
> A mystical African atmosphere

A cultural beat on an African drum
Like the beat of the heart when life began ...

A Benjamin Zephaniah poetry performance is charged
with vitality, rhythm, humour, the release of frustration and
a well-developed entertaining and individual style. It is not
surprising that his performances usually attract large
audiences of both black and white young adults from different backgrounds. Recently he launched a ten-piece touring
band to back, support and enhance his work. His second
book of poems, *The Dread Affair*, should also contribute to
his continued development. Here is an example of the strong
mix of satire and social protest in Benjamin Zephaniah's
poetry, from 'Dis Policeman Keeps on Kicking me to Death':

Like a bat from hell he comes at night
to work his evil plan
although he goes to church on Sunday
he's a sinner man,
like a thief in de dark he take me to de
place where he just left
and when him get me in der
he is kicking me to death.
Dis policeman, dis policeman
dis policeman keeps on kicking me to death ...

Once it had been exposed in public performance, once the
movements with their committed feeling expressed in black-
culture style had combined with memorized words, the new
dynamic poetry began to excite, stir and inspire new performers. More and more young black poets began to launch
themselves upon the public with this new word-art. Each
aspect of it had become part of a whole message. And the
form called 'dub poetry' brings black people together. It
offers a voice which is cultural, political and social. It facili-
tates expression of long-stored rejection, marginalization,
frustration and a sense of continued deprivation. It tones up
self-reliance and burnishes a self-image. And, in releasing and
unifying, it enhances confidence of identity.

Looking at work written within a span of about ten years we can identify inner turmoil, confusion and resistance. In the early 1970s a schoolboy in his early teens wrote his 'Vivian Usherwood' poems. Published by Centerprise and low-priced, the book sold thousands of copies and continues to sell. Metaphorically, movingly, his poems arouse in a subjective way. Listen to 'My Name is I Don't know':

My name is I don't know.
I wish it was something else.
I work so hard trying to keep my world clean,
Then along comes some unkind creature
and drops a litter or two,
Then I have to clean it up.
Along comes someone else and does the same,
So I have no sleep ...

In 1977, while I worked as writer-in-residence in a London comprehensive school, a 16-year-old girl, Ramona Sealy, wrote this short short story 'Life Story of a Woman':

I was brought up a slave. When I was twelve I was sold to a kind master. He treated me well. I enjoyed it. I was a slave who served the master his meals and got his things for hunting. I was carrying my master's meal when I dropped it on the floor. The cook told my master. He said if it happened again I would be severely punished. It was night time I made up my mind to run away. I escaped for a year and a day. I came back. I asked for my freedom. My master gave me my freedom. I said, where can I go? What can I do? You taught me only to be a slave. Teach me now to be free.

In 1982, through women's issues explored at the same school (Vauxhall Manor) a play, *Motherland*, was developed from interviews that a former pupil, Marcia Smith, carried out with West Indian women of her mother's generation in the local community, working with Elyse Dodgson who directed and guided the dramatization. The play was first performed by Oval House. In Act 1, after West Indian women have been refused accommodation for various reasons (obviously untrue), another door is tried.

LANDLADY 4: You've been walking all day and your feet hurt. You want a room. Well, I'm sorry, we don't allow niggers in this house.
(*The door is shut. A knock.*)

LANDLADY 5: (*opens door*) Yes, love.

WOMAN 5: I've come back for that room you promised me.

LANDLADY 5: Sorry, I've already given it to somebody else.
(*The West Indian women sing.*)

SINGER 1: Searchin, wow, I'm searchin.

SINGER 2: Tryin to find a place to rest.

SINGER 3: Searchin, keep on searchin.

SINGER 4: England, you put me to your test ...

In the same year Dave Martin, another teenager, wrote in 'Us Dreads':

In a dis ya skool
us dreads rool.
... When exam come
some dreads run
lose out in de enn
but us dreads still frienn.

About the same time Beverley Skyers was writing 'Run Riot':

A brethren throws a brick
an' a bull get lick
A sister throws a stone
an' more bull come down.
Babylon tek out dem riot shiel'
but dat nah stop dem from bleed ...

The year 1984 saw the Sixth Black Youth Annual Penmanship Awards promoted by ACER. Writing on 'My Experience of Being of Mixed Parentage in Britain/What Makes a Black Person Black?', 20-year-old overall winner Jenneba Sie Jalloh wrote in 'A Subtle Shade of Black':

Never one or the other

Fighting to be one, wanting to be one, Needing to be one
But scared. Always there, but never there
Who am I? Where do I belong? ...

Some Strong Influences

Caribbean writers inherited the richness of both Caribbean
'Nation Language' and standard English, and their work
reflects that. Look at extracts of work from the Caribbean's
best-known international poets. Edward Kamau Brathwaite's
famous 'Rites' (on cricket) has:

> ... You see dat shot?' the people was shoutin;
> Jesus Chrise, man, wunna see dat shot?' ...

and his 'Sun Poem' has:

> ... when my songs were first heard in the voice of the coot of
> the owl
> hillaby soufriere and kilimanjaro were standing towards
> me ...

And Derek Walcott in his poem 'Spoiler's Return', about a
dead calypso singer, says:

> ... Tell Desperadoes when you reach the hill,
> I decompose, but I composing still ...

while in his 'Port of Spain' he writes:

> ... Midsummer stretches before me with a cat's yawn ...

Listen to legendary folklorist Jamaican Louise Bennett in her
'Proverbs':

> 'Sweet mout fly
> Follow coffin go a hole' ...

and master of the folk story-poem, Paul Keens-Douglas of
Trinidad, in his 'When Moon Shine':

... De man stink, stink ah rum,
An' come pushin' up in me face ...

The Rastafarians too have now made their impact on the
language. They have brought in their 'I-and-I', meaning both
'Jah' and 'I-human'. They have reinterpreted words (Jamaica
becomes 'Jah-mek-yah', meaning 'Jah makes here' or 'Jah is/
was made here').

Yet a little noted aspect of Caribbean 'Nation Language' in
the literature is its use of all-time-is-now: the language disre-
gards past and future tenses and brings its knowing into the
present. It is not 'Buddy came and saw me last night' but
'Buddy come see me last night', not 'I will be going to the
market on Saturday' but 'I go market Saturday.' Louise
Bennett worked this linguistic trait into her early *Anancy
Stories*, as in this piece from 'Anancy an' Crab' (1957): 'Wen
evenin' come, Anancy goh to de ole lady fe him pay an she tell
him sey dat him we haffe fine out her name fus ...' John
Hearne, the Jamaican novelist, has used this form to excellent
effect in his story 'At the Stelling'. In my own short story
'Canteen Girl' I brought the form into standard English: 'She
stands over me. I wonder if she will speak: this slim figure in
white cap and overall. She doesn't look at me, not straight
anyway ...'

Another important point is that with its heavy reliance on
sound, 'Nation Language' searches to discover how it should
settle down in written form. More and more the words
appear on the page with sharp, clear Afro-Caribbean sounds.
For example, 'me' has become 'mi'; 'for', which used to be
'fe', has become 'fi'; 'into', which used to be 'ena' or 'eena',
may be 'in-a' or 'inna'; 'can't' may be 'caan', 'cyaan' or
'cahn', etc. Particular forms have a way of recurring and may
well become standard usage.

Among the new generations born in Britain, or those who
have merely grown up here, the different Caribbean voices
have come together to form black British speech. All-Islands
speech characteristics have merged into something harmo-
nious, like the West Indies cricket team. Rastafari and Bob

Marley have contributed their influences. But, naturally, the local use of standard English has made the biggest mark on British black speech, whether it be London or a regional variant of Bradford or Cardiff speech. But what used to be a Trinidadian's 'I ain' doing that' has become 'I na do dat.' And that 'na' used to be Jamaican 'noh'. It is interesting too that children born in Britain have often found the speech of their Caribbean-born parents amusing. Listen to 17-year-old Dorial Brown's poem, 'Girl', about what her Barbadian mother said:

> Girl, why you want to go out every night
> Every night God sends
> No, you is a girl
> Stay home and wash your clothes
> Learn to cook
> You is a girl
> You want to spin the broad road
> Like them two she-cats yonder
> Not my girl.

Surprised to see that their children born in Britain have developed a pride in 'Nation Language', parents born in the Caribbean are often horrified too. Conditioned to believe that their own language is 'bush talk' and 'bad' and 'down-grading', the parents want their children to use the language that will bring them qualifications and achievements. These should not be denied them, surely, but the children do not want to be denied their balance. For that Afro-Caribbean spirit that desires full expression of both identity and culture style maintains an increased and intensified momentum.

The literature declares the fact of a two-language heritage. From 'Patois', 'dialect', 'Creole', the people's language has come now to be called 'Nation Language'. It may well soon be called 'Caribbean' to identify itself more accurately. Champion of the new term is the poet and Senior Lecturer in History at the University of the West Indies, Dr Edward Kamau Brathwaite. He has reminded us that when newly arrived Africans found themselves in the Caribbean in the early days, they always identified themselves as belonging to this or that 'nation'.

While Caribbean mainstream poetry has been strongly influenced by British writing traditions, popular Caribbean-British poetry has its parents in the folk, calypso and integrated jazz blues traditions. A prominent feature is the traditional calypso humour. It is that essential characteristic of the calypsonian genius: the eye that finds what is comic in an event, situation or crisis, whether local, national or international, or simply in a man-and-woman relationship, shouting for 'ol' talk'. And it teases it up to public attention and gets it inescapably focused in an outrageous exposure or sheer scandal of a song. Listen to Jimi Rand in his poem 'Nock Nock Oo Nock E Nock', which is about a national figure, the Rt Hon. Enoch Powell, MP, who has insisted that his life's work is dedicated to a rejection of black people's presence:

> ... Nock nock – nock nock,
> badoombadoom nock nock
> ... badoombadoom nock badoom nock
> Who dat; a who dat nock?
> E nock
> ... E nock gwine sen ya back ...

See also how John Agard exposes stereotyping in his 'Palm Tree King':

> ... Because I come from the West Indies
> certain people in England seem to think
> I is a expert on palm trees
> ... I does smile cool as seabreeze
> and say to dem
> which specimen
> you interested in
> ... Tell me what you want to know
> How tall a palm tree does grow?
> ... like if a American tourist with a camera
> take 9 minutes to climb a coconut tree
> how long a English tourist without a camera
> would take to climb the same coconut tree? ...

Attempts made to popularize and celebrate black-culture
subjects through poetry found and published in the anthology *Bluefoot Traveller* (1976) managed to stir little response
in new writers. Yet Faustin Charles's poem 'Viv' and my own
'Batsman-with-Music Sobers' still support C. L. R. James in
his comment that 'West Indians crowding to Tests bring with
them the whole past history and future hopes of the islands.'
In cricket everybody, and the black player himself, knows he
can achieve a perfect performance, and does. It is well understood that decisions taken about his success or failure will not
be subjected to any behind-the-scenes 'umpiring'. Success
here has the stuff of heightened poetry, surely. Similarly,
Hugh Hailson Boatswain's music celebration poems 'The
Bongo Man' and 'Dub Rock' do not seem to have caught
anybody's eye either. Errol Nelson's 'Ekome Feemo Hewa-
leyo' too still begs emulation:

> ... We are the sons and daughters
> of histories buried in secret places.
> And we dance to a beat,
> that is the dark pulse of Africa.
> We will dance, the dance of birds
> gliding from tree top to tree top
> under a clear blue sky.
> ... We will dance, a dance of war
> that you may understand
> how futile it is to hate ...

Adaptation

This phase of the new relationship embraces, in a going and
coming over mountains of difficult history, attempts to
adapt, to find a new security.

Archie Markham's poem 'Love at No. 13' begins:

> her nurse's fingers burn
> in a grip that has known
> a cutlass ...

Grace Nichols's 'I is a Long Memoried Woman' reflects:

Heavy with child
belly
an arc
of black moon
I squat over
dry plantain leaves
and command the earth
to receive you
in my name
in my blood
to receive you
my curled bean
my tainted
perfect child
my bastard fruit
my seedling
my sea grape
my strange mulatto
my little bloodling ...

Creswell Durrant's 'Colours' (about the Notting Hill riots) comments:

... Saw once the silence of the street,
converge impolitely at five in the borough council morning
on two crossing sweepers black and white
filling their brotherhood at a milk machine.

Then, in 'Two Men in the Slums', RAPP shows that a certain way of life is soon fatal:

... on his own, roamed the streets alone
Looking for life, finding strife, on the run
For fun, stole a gun ...
Take some risks ...
one night instead, found himself dead.

School-leaving results often give black parents reason to believe that both the teaching and the general atmosphere of Britain 'switches off' their children or fails to 'switch them on'. Born in England and living in South London, Leslie

Anthony Goffe published an article in 1981 entitled 'An Education for a Black Briton'. Goffe was puzzled by the fact that unemployment was 'twice as high among blacks as whites, with police SUS convictions ten times as high'. He was also confused about whether he was a 'black Englishman' or not. He had been informed by a teacher, 'Just because one is born in England that does not make one an Englishman.' But if his 'black skin and brown eyes could never be English, how then was it that white-skinned, blue-eyed Englishmen could go to South Africa and become African?'

Born and brought up in Scotland, one of the four black women poets in *A Dangerous Knowing* (1984), Jackie Kay, begins her poem 'So You Think I'm a Mule?':

> 'Where do you come from?'
> 'I'm from Glasgow.'
> 'Glasgow?'
> 'Uh huh. Glasgow.'
> The white face hesitates
> the eyebrows raise
> the mouth opens
> then snaps shut
> incredulous ...

In the same anthology Barbara Burford responds to her British black experience in 'Introspection Blues':

> ... There is a kindliness
> more deadly than hate
> lifting each painfully
> healed scab.
> Spreading a stinging ointment
> of charm ...

Coolly, in 'You Hear Bout?', Valerie Bloom asks questions:

> Yuh hear bout de people dem arres
> Fi bun dung de Asian people dem house?
> Yuh hear bout de policeman dem lock up

Fi beat up de black bwoy widout a cause?
Yuh hear bout de MP dem sack because im refuse fi help
im coloured constituents ...?

Searching for relief in drugs, like lack of confidence in elected leadership, appears with the recurring confusion of identity. Memories of the Caribbean surface in 'Darkness Night' by Jamaican-born Londoner Desmond Johnson:

... bawling
'Darkness! Night!'
I took out a spliff
from my cigarette box
light it up
puff pull swallow
puff pull swallow
repeatedly
until the beach caught fire ...

Among the 1984 crop of new books was David Dabydeen's volume of poems in Guyanese voices, *Slave Song*, which won him the Commonwealth Poetry Prize. There was my anthology of British Black poetry, *News for Babylon*, too and, before that, Ziggi Alexander's and Audrey Dewjee's biography of Mary Seacole.

Industrious 23-year-old Desmond Johnson makes the poetry scene brighter with his newly established Akira Press, already in the process of publishing a number of little-known black poets. Thanks to leading black publishers New Beacon Books and Bogle-L'Ouverture – which started it all – along with Centerprise, Race Today, the Black Ink Collective, Women's, Community and other small presses, new black writers' work has begun to see the light of day and continues to do so. For the black presence here is good for Britain.

The black presence in Britain teaches and learns. It strives for greater fulfilment. It exposes white people to inescapable racial differences and to their own tribal attitudes and shortcomings, while it generates a new dimension to their awareness. Black people's presence in Britain encourages a mental expansiveness that can help white people to absorb the reality of a society that is like a miniature planet, to be harmonized into a reality of cultural pluralism. The British black cultural thrust has truly arrived at an exciting phase. Yet it needs to ensure that it is directed towards neither a dead end nor a precipice.

Is the Scene Set for a Developed British Black Culture?

Caribbean novelists based themselves in Britain in the 1950s and brought Caribbean writing to the world's attention. By the 1970s, however, one after the other they had disappeared from the scene. Michael Anthony and E. R. Braithwaite went back to the Caribbean. Andrew Salkey took up a teaching post in the USA. Samuel Selvon went to live in Canada. Though V. S. Naipaul has remained in England, and has become very famous internationally, he was never one to be involved with Britain's black communities. Wilson Harris and George Lamming too have remained here but are not prominently active either. And, interestingly, since new books from these writers have stopped coming out, up to now no new black novelist living in Britain has had an equivalent impact. But a big change has taken place.

The attitude to life and language and humour of Samuel Selvon's characters of the 1950s has changed. The new generations have become more intensely politicized and more race- and culture-conscious. Impelled by struggle, the people have activated themselves in a drive that seems bent on fulfilling their racial reality and their part of a diverse wholeness.

They take all kinds of cultural, historical and social facts and data about themselves into education, into the arts, into politics and into the social life of Britain. They have set up spare-time supplementary schools to help their children. They have established their yearly Caribbean Carnival in city streets and keep up their open celebration of all cultures. With their week-long fourth annual International Bookfair of Radical Black and Third World Books, with its forums, readings, debates, discussions, Caribbean people in Britain have set up another vital and invigorating cultural event in London life.

With the impact of 'Nation Language' and culture-style poetry, the broad black masses have been stirred in a new way. The people have swiftly developed the habit of coming together for events. And participation grows at community grassroots level.

Study groups and workshops for the various arts have proliferated. Writers' workshops happened to become popular at about the same time as a general interest in working-class autobiographical writing emerged as one of many community arts activities around Britain. Black writers' workshops developed their own approach, offered liberty to write in oral language – 'Nation Language'. A new freedom, this! It filled writers with a sense of triumph over pedantic English teachers and editors; they knew they would never give the pedants a chance to find fault with their work. And the people are spurred to go to black theatre, to see and hear themselves reflected in their own ways of speech. And just as musicians, dancers and artists from other parts of the black world come with their contributions too, the film makers struggle to play their role.

The people have adjusted their self-image. They have long rejected European criteria as standards by which to judge their own art. The established exclusivity of European's artistic excellence is now seen as both prohibitive and irrelevant. Particularly, that superior and totalitarian stance of standard English has been swept aside. Yet as this cultural renewal gathers momentum, naturally serious omissions emerge. And the question of a developed British black culture stirs mixed hopes, doubts and stubborn realities.

Black people are still alerted by threats to their survival concealed in racism, by habits of historical non-sharing, hurt and injustice and by gunboat soldiering and policing methods far from dead. They feel that everything to reduce them lurks in racism. They see racism as the worst kind of in-built unfeeling and greed, which deals in seizing the lion's share, in ways that range from the avaricious to the deadly, and is helplessly driven by a compulsion to have the light of blacks to shine with. So white people's ethics have to be constantly monitored and policed. Yet at the same time this obsession threatens to set its own continuous preoccupation as its own trap.

Just as white has responded to black as subversive, black children have come to see white culture as subversive. Caribbean-British schoolchildren have developed a way of deliberately 'switching off' in lessons they see as 'white' and similarly opt out of taking exams because their group decides this is a 'white thing'. Black people need to see how much they unconsciously encourage and nurture failure and a ghetto mentality. Unless we can work to make a reality of people belonging to people and knowledge belonging to everybody, we are surely sunk.

Black people need to keep an eye open for a kind of 'domination hypnosis' that keeps domination strategies working. Racism still has the victim activated by the offender, not by anything independent that the offended has started. Even after slavery ended, when in the 1830s the British Government gave slave owners £20 million to set nearly 1 million Caribbean people free as compensation for the loss of a no-wages workforce and 'private property', freedom was only restored, not given. Already a birthright, freedom is like sunshine, air, water and the earth. Freedom can only be hindered. That word 'given', which implies magnanimity and goodness, is all part of the big bluff, and the arrogance, of domination psychology.

The Gaps and Some Possibilities

'Dub poetry', with its intensity and shock value, has done its job so well that it engenders imitators who swallow their model whole. The imitators seem to believe firmly that black poetry can only be a protest against racism and deprivation. And, unfortunately, listeners who hear it – and are perhaps impressed by poetry for the first time – seem to arrive at a similar evaluation.

British black poetry should not want to be stuck with this one dimension. It should want to expand its awareness. It could still work wonders with the 'dub' form, using fresh themes. For example, the poetry shows little signs of exploring relationships, or real personal experience, or black culture's myths and legends, or the natural universe, or a celebration of anything. It is in the creative imagination that new forms and plans and inventions are found. Black writers need to stimulate that imaginative experience. They need to remember that Caribbean countries have not yet evolved new economic and social structures to replace the old colonial ones effectively. Caribbean nations have not yet dreamed up the good life for their people. While they may have invented steelpan music as the most effective twentieth-century musical instrument, they have explored hardly any depths of the Caribbean psyche with it or composed any appropriate, top-class, original music to play on it. A workable plan for educational, economic, industrial or social change could be better than a great poem.

Equally, the writing suffers from a lack of informed and creative critics who could show their appreciation of different levels of perception and of the value of Caribbean continuity. Editors of magazines and newspaper arts pages too could devise fresh, creative ways to arouse greater interest in black writers and to stimulate both a wider appreciation of their work and finer skills in the word-arts. Along with British black contemporary work, they could find ways to introduce writings from, say, *Caribbean Voices*, that large anthology of poetry edited by John Figueroa, who now lives in England. They could also stir awareness and examination of the ways in which the English language uses the word 'black'. For example, is 'blackmail' a subtle way unconsciously to suggest to the world that the black male exists by criminal extortion? And because 'blackleg' is not 'whiteleg' or 'halfleg' or 'crookedleg' or any other 'leg', does that particular word set up an unconscious image of anyone with black legs as a traitor or swindler? Also, when we see that the language does not use 'non-black', has the word 'non-white' come from the unconscious of apartheid supporters, subtly suggesting acquiescence in black people's extinction and non-existence?

Afro-Caribbean and British black writing displays outrage at abuse and exclusion; it expresses resistance and outcry; it reflects, redefines, reassesses, reclaims and restores. It exposes the experience of a merely-to-be-human survival struggle. The writing impresses with its immense energy, wanting to create that expanded mind and spirit that we call human fulfilment.

Part Two

Language and Society

6

Creole as a Language of Power and Solidarity

ANSEL WONG

Second-generation blacks are in crisis solely if judged from a non-political, non-historical viewpoint – only in that case can their behaviour be labelled pathological. With political insight, however, it can be seen to be a dynamic resistance that – if one adds insights from an historical perspective – can *then* be regarded as cultural resistance, aggressively expressed in its interface with mainstream society. Such resistance finds its artistic focus in language and music, as we have seen. Ansel Wong points out the inherent racism in British society. Creole, as a source of strength and pride, and with its vocabularly transformed by Rasta, enables blacks to fight back.

> The world of the minority group member is shaped not only by . . . individual experiences, but also by group responses that are passed along in the stream of culture.
>
> *(Simpson and Yinger, 1965)*

Any understanding of the black communities in the UK, and specifically the important role that language plays, can be grasped only within the context of an historical overview of the British black presence and a critical analysis of some of the cultural and political antecedents of that presence. In seeking to understand the importance of Creole to the black community, it is also important to appreciate the nature of

the relationship between the black community and the dominant society as well as the tension and conflicts within the
black community itself.

The British black presence can be traced back to the mid-
sixteenth century (Walvin, 1971, 1973; Scobie, 1972; Shyllon, 1974; Lorimer, 1978), when blacks were brought to
London as retainers, servants and sailors. By the mid-eigh-
teenth century about 3 per cent of London's population was
of African heritage, concentrated mostly around Wapping, St
Giles and Clerkenwell.

It is important to concern ourselves with this historical
perspective if only to correct 'the tendency to pull race out of
the internal dynamic of British society, and to repress its
history' and thus to view the crisis of race in our society as a
continuing one with a long history and not as something that
has suddenly happened as a result of recent immigration by
peoples from the Caribbean and the Indian subcontinent.
Without this historical overview there is a danger of regard-
ing the importance and relevance of race as 'an external virus
somehow injected into the body politic ... [It is] a matter of
policy whether we can deal with it or not ... not a matter of
politics' (Hall, 1978).

The concern in past centuries, as now, centered on the
question of numbers. This is illustrated by the Act of Privy
Council of 11 August 1576, stating: 'Her Majestie, understanding that there are of late divers blackamoors brought to
this realm, of which kinde of people there are already too
manie, considering how God hath blessed this land with great
increase of people of our own nation ... those kinde of people
should be sent forth of the land ...' Repatriation was thus
seen as the solution to this growing black presence, a presence that Edward Long, the Enoch Powell of the eighteenth
century and, ironically, a Jamaican planter, saw as a grave
menace. He wrote in 1772: 'We must agree with those who
have declared that the public good of this kingdom requires
that some restraint should be laid on the unnatural increase
of blacks imported into it.'

There were fears then that (to put it in the terms in which people thought) the bestial and uncivilized nature of the black man would contaminate the lily-white purity of the British populace and act as an 'alien wedge'. Many people openly expressed their hostility to these 'divers blackamoors' because of their fear of being raped or murdered on the streets of London (Walvin, 1971). The 'immigrant footpad' and 'suspected person' were popular bogeys then as they are now. Thus it is important to recognize that in looking at the black experience one must be mindful of these historical relations that have 'central features in the formation of Britain's material prosperity and dominance, as they are now central themes in English culture and in popular and official ideologies' (Hall, 1978), central themes that influence each individual today in evolving 'group responses that are passed along in the stream of culture'.

The most recent wave of black settlers was a response to the economic demands of the British state and the social and economic conditions 'back home'. The beginning of this period of settlement occurred in the 1940s and 1950s, and the growth of this movement of people was determined principally by the interplay of free market forces. Thus periods of economic expansion resulted in an increase in immigration and periods of economic recession in a resulting decline (Peach, 1968).

In accepting this analysis it is important to realize that Britain's economic growth and power were founded on the slave trade and the plantation economies of its Empire – in short, on the colonialist and imperialist connection that determined the destiny of millions of black workers (Williams, 1964). The main effects of colonialism in the Caribbean were under-development and the creation of a reserve army of labour on which Britain drew to fuel its economic boom.

The Caribbean countries were in essence city-states revolving around the economic axis of metropolitan Britain. But within the region itself there was also large-scale migration of labour. Thousands of Caribbean workers migrated to work on the Panama Canal, the banana plantations of Costa Rica, the fruit farms of the Southern states of America and the sugar plantations of Cuba. With the USA a system of contract labour was developed, but with the passing of the Walters–McCarran Act of 1952, which applied a rigid quota system to Caribbean workers, Britain became the main recipient of the area's surplus labour.

There was also the deliberate recruitment of labour from the Caribbean by London Transport, the National Health Service and the British Hotels and Restaurants Association. Thus economic forces and the colonial relationship determined the type of work reserved for these migrant workers, and this meant that black workers were found mainly in unskilled and low-status jobs that the indigenous white workers were unwilling to accept. This, in turn, meant that the black workers' labour power became vital to the economic bloodstream of British society.

As they were situated within the non-growth sectors of the industrial economy, these black workers were concentrated in the major cities and in the worst housing. Economically and socially trapped in the decaying inner cities, they came into direct contact with all the structural contradictions and deficiencies of this late industrial/capitalist society. 'To put it crudely, the economic profit from immigration had gone to capital, the social cost had gone to labour, but the resulting conflict between the two had been mediated by a common "ideology" of racism' (Sivanandan, 1976).

For many black workers, still nurturing positive feelings towards the 'mother country', it was a rude awakening to experience racism and to discover that British society is endemically racist. Manifestations of this racism – individual and institutional – cut across class lines. The most dramatic evidence of it occurred during the race riots of Notting Hill and Nottingham in 1958, during which a black man, Kelso Cochrane, died.

The increasing hostility to the black presence and the economic downturn resulted in the introduction of varying forms of immigration control, which effectively negotiated the transition of the status of black Commonwealth citizens from that of British citizens to that of contract labourers (Sivanandan, 1976). The growth of Powellism and 'respectable' political activity against the black presence led to an increasing tension in British society between labour and capital. Inevitably, the black workers became the scapegoats. As new recruits to the labour force, they were perceived as the cause of the crisis. Thus 'race punctuates and periodizes the crisis' for it is 'the lens through which people come to perceive that a crisis is developing. It is the framework through which the crisis is experienced' (Hall, 1978).

The black workers' experience of the crisis was also perceived within a racial context. Despite being at the receiving end of it, they nevertheless cultivated a dogged determination to struggle on in the hope that conditions would improve for their children, who would be native to the country. But their children, although they are British-born, are also experiencing the crisis, both in the sheltered environment of the school and in the more overtly hostile neighbourhoods where they live.

It is therefore to these young people that one must turn to understand the importance of language as an edifice on which is constructed racial pride and power as well as a defence against the assimilationist encroachment of the dominant society. It is these young lions, who have 'come to know, in our short while, the razor route of wretchedness, the alphabet of terror', who have invested Creole with new dimensions and meanings, for it is around these young people that the ethos of resistance is developing. One of the principal features of this resistance is the ability to communicate in a unique form of language, invariably described as Creole, Patois, Jamaica Talk, dialect, 'Backayard' lingo, etc.

These black adolescents form an urban sub-proletariat removed from the apex of power because of their relationship with capital and their ethnicity. This relationship, situated in a highly industrialized capitalist society, determines their culture and normative values, which are in turn shaped around distinctive activities and central communal concerns.

Thus they articulate and practise distinct and separate cultural responses to their material and social status through their dress, political allegiances, survival strategies and language.

In examining how language is used as an appropriate medium for this symbolic and interactive resistance, it is necessary to turn to the Rastafarian Movement, as a study of its importance to black adolescents will reveal how Creole or Patois soon gained prominence as the most concrete expression of the community's power and sense of solidarity. Competence in Jamaican Patois, increasingly validated and nurtured by the growing popularity of reggae music, developed into one of the most visible signs of this allegiance, and as it became embedded in, and central to, the emerging black urban subculture the language started also to acquire characteristics and features unique to the British black experience.

The popular appeal of the Rastafarian Movement is seen by oppressed blacks as a 'primary form of resistance' to the physical and historical realities of the society that dominates them. It is considered 'an indelible link between the resistance of the Maroons, the Pan-Africanist appeal of Marcus Garvey, the practices of Cumima and Pocomania, the materialist and historical analysis of Walter Rodney and the internationalized reggae sounds of defiance' (Campbell, 1979).

The popular, media-packed image of a Rasta is a *ganja*-smoking cultist, speaking in an untutored but quaint tongue, who believes in the deity of Haile Selassie and is for ever in a drugged stupor, dreaming of the millennial return to Ethiopia or rocking until the wee hours to a monotonous beat. Without a historical and political analysis that takes account of a political response to racism and exploitation, the emphasis on specific cultural manifestations often leads one to regard the Rasta youth as a petty criminal. The most revealing example of such a response was published in the *Reading Evening Post* under the headline 'YARD ALERT ON BLACK MAFIA'. The article ran:

Scotland Yard has alerted police forces in England and Wales about an infiltration threat by a West Indian Mafia organization called Rastafarians. It is an international crime ring specializing in drugs, prostitution, extortion, protection, subversion and blackmail ... They are known to police and intelligence organizations on both sides of the Atlantic as being active in organizing industrial unrest. (Press Gang, 1978)

A study of the political socialization of black youths has shown that among Afro-Caribbeans there is a growing number who possess 'an ethnically specific conceptualization of political reality' and are therefore likely to embrace unconventional and illegitimate methods of political action (Phizacklea, 1975). The majority of this group are turning to the Rastafarian Movement because of 'its flexible and all-embracing (the combination of the material and the transcendent) nature: the emphasis on slavery, colonialism and the African homeland, denuded of the transcendent, could become the means of expression of a black nationalist politics' (Miles, 1978). For many it is a visible way of articulating their discontent, of asserting their struggle for justice and liberation, of publicly confronting all that this society stands for. Significantly, it is reggae, a music that is 'the spiritual expression of a historical experience of the Afro-Jamaican' (Johnson, 1976), reflecting the condition and actual life experience of black youth and providing it with an ideology of liberation, that acts as the initial attraction. Thus young black people agree with Bunny Wailer when he sings:

To be trapped and caught and then taken before judge and jury
Pleading before men who seem to have no mercy ...

Battering down sentence
Fighting against convictions ...

or with Bob Marley, whose song highlights the destructive nature of a capitalist society in which viciousness and competitiveness result in each man's being the potential enemy of the other (Hylton, 1975):

Man to man is so unjust
You don't know who to trust.
Your worst enemy could be your best friend,
Your best friend, your worst enemy.

For black youth in London Rastafari is both a cultural and a political response to racism as well as a geophysical and psychic journey into self, a self that is under continuous attack and prone to negative labelling. Consequently, the young person embracing 'Rasta' is also entering into a further stage in a search for psychic reference points in consolidating his or her identity as a black person. 'Being a Rastafarian gives an awareness of being black in a white-dominated world – not as a minority group, but as a minority elite. A positive value is attached to racial identity. The Rastas have elevated and glorified blackness' (Cashmore, 1977).

Rastafari thus offers young people a convenient mechanism by which they can demonstrate their cultural and political resistance to assimilation in order to ward off attempts, by the state and its agencies of social control, to infiltrate, to create an Afro-Saxon. It is a timely, 'home-grown' ideology of liberation, which contains the social, cultural and political forces that they can use to harness, adapt, legitimize and develop all the social practices and cultural elements of their sub-proletariat status and roots culture – aspects considered shameful and subnormal by British society.

Unlike the black Muslims in the USA who reinforce and recreate the materialist and capitalist base of American society of which racism is an integral component, the Rastafarian Movement rejects all that is 'Babylon' by emphasizing the subversive rhythms and practices of the black masses, so that in the end it becomes not a fanatical religious cult but an aggressive, uncompromising assertion of their racial and class identity – 'a preliminary movement of symbolic protest against the subordinate structural and ideological position of black people in England' (Miles, 1978). For the black adolescents in our secondary schools it offers a cultural renaissance by which they can break the bonds of their more accommo-

dating parents and the race relations industry by transform-
ing a situation of extreme cultural dependence, 'downpression', the true meanings of Rasta into a state of great
autonomy and freedom through 'overstanding'.

In effect, then, many of these black youths have, literally
and ritualistically, clothed themselves in an excessive and
aggressive individualism without any loyalty or allegiance to
their captive society. Bongo Jerry, a Rastafarian poet,
expresses these sentiments when he writes:

> I booked no passage to come
> Paid no plane fare
> They bid me applaud when Jews
> Shout ZION
> Yet what am I doing here?
> I am a captive.

Such an ideology provides an ideal framework for harnessing
the discontent, 'the razor route of wretchedness' and 'the
alphabet of terror', that seems to characterize the experiences
of inner-city black youths. And it is this ideology that has
legitimized the importance of Creole, that has made it a
dialect with a gunboat.

In a sense, the adoption of Creole by many black adolescents is also a reaction against the dominant language –
standard English, interpreted as the main thrust of the integration of the 'dark strangers' and 'alienated youth' through
the schools – which is seen by many as militating against
black people.

An examination of the vocabulary of the language will
show that the concept of 'whiteness' and the word 'white' has
134 synonyms, of which only ten are negative in their use
(e.g., 'whitewash', 'ashen', 'wan'). The emotions, meanings
and values attached to these negative leanings are also very
mild. The concept of 'blackness' and the word 'black', on the
other hand, have 120 synonyms, of which sixty are clearly
negative and unfavourable (e.g. 'blot', 'smudge', 'malignant',
'foul') and an additional twenty have direct reference to a
racial group ('negro', 'nigger', 'darky', etc.).

Thus the language of instruction and literature is saturated with words, concepts, idioms, sayings that have strong and loaded values and nuances that suggest, directly or indirectly, notions of racial superiority, inferiority and suppression. Martin Luther King (1968) describes the situation thus:

A white lie is better than a black lie. The most degenerate member of a family is the 'black sheep', not the 'white sheep'. Ossie Davis has suggested that maybe the English language should be 're-constructed' so that teachers will not be forced to teach the Negro child sixty ways to despise himself and thereby perpetuate his false sense of inferiority and the white child 134 ways to adore himself and thereby perpetuate his false sense of superiority.

These notions of racial dominance and superiority were formerly reinforced in the schools, where the languages of Third World peoples were denigrated and marginalized. Schools are only now beginning to come to terms with their marginalization of the languages of black people, once defined as 'ethnic minority languages' or 'community or heritage languages' or by the more racist phrase 'jungle talk'. However, the most graphic illustration of the way in which these prejudiced attitudes are reinforced is the following text from *Today's English Book* 2, published in 1974:

Farther away still, east of the Mediterranean, all semblance of what we know as writing vanishes, and notices, papers and place-names appear to have been printed by a demented, ink-soaked spider crawling over the pages. What would you do if confronted by

It seems impossible to us that anyone could turn what appears to be the idle scribbling of a half-witted child of one year into speech, and yet any Arab or Chinese would be able to make

the correct mouth noise from these scripts and obey the instruction 'No smoking allowed'.

It is such racist attitudes to any language spoken by people of colour, as well as the racist overtones and nuances of the English language itself, that have contributed to the phenomenon of many second-generation black youths acquiring linguistic competence in a Jamaican Patois that is assuming many aspects of Cockney, which makes the end product more a London Jamaican language than a Jamaican Jamaican. For many black adolescents, especially the followers of Rastafari, this Patois is a powerful social and political mantle which, by emphasizing its own subversive rhythms and 'foreignness', becomes an aggressive and proud assertion of racial and class identities. It can also be seen as a process by which extreme cultural dependence is transmuted into greater autonomy and independence primarily through their use of Patois to create linguistic barriers. The result is that the language is invested with a legitimacy that both their parents and the dominant society have consistently resisted.

This subversion of the English language is best illustrated by words and syllables that are altered to create new forms that have different cultural and political overtones when used by the black speaker. The following English words and their Patois equivalents, called Afro-Lingua, illustrate this process:

English	Afro-Lingua
unity	Inity
politics	politricks
system	shitstem
understand	overstand
oppression	downpression

This is a deliberate and conscious move by black youths to make their speech more relevant to their perceptions of their lives and their struggles with the dominant society. Steeped in both the biblical and the Rastafarian concept of redemption, black Patois speakers are trying to forge for themselves a medium that can be used to underpin their quest for unity and togetherness. For the black rebels Patois is the principal and private bearer of their cultural capital. It is one way of asserting individuality, an assertion that in its aggressive expression often invites responses of annoyance and dislike, not unlike the dogmatic attitude of a secondary school head who boasted (Morris, 1977):

> Should I create a black curriculum? Should I put Creole on the timetable? Over my dead body, and the majority of my parents would cheer me to the skies. They want their children to get jobs. I will not even allow Patois plays in the school. It must not be elevated to linguistic status at the expense of English.

By adopting such a dogmatic attitude towards Patois and by refusing to legitimize its use as a language in its own right, schools negate the black child's linguistic competence. The effect of this is that the teaching of English in most schools has become a process of dismantling the child's linguistic competence rather than adding a second language to his London Jamaican dialect. Again, a conflict relationship is nurtured in the classroom. As Edwards (1979) says:

> The language of school and teachers is steeped in descriptive labels like 'proper English' and 'good grammar' while the way that working-class children speak is all too often dismissed as 'wrong', 'sloppy' and 'ugly' ... this is tantamount to saying that the school cannot accept these children, their families or their community for what they are. It is hardly surprising, therefore, that the main influence on a child is his peer group and a frequent response to the school's criticism of the child's speech – explicit or implicit – is to continue in his present speech patterns, reinforced by his peers, rather than to respond to his teachers' exhortations to 'speak properly'.

Resistance thus takes the form of the deliberate cultivation of Patois and its continued use, to the annoyance of teachers and the delight of black students: 'Mrs L. she don't like us to say anything. We always have to speak proper English so that she can understand. We are speaking proper. But the way she carry on ... as if we can't talk at all. She's really stuck up' (Payne, 1978).

In using the dominant language, English, which is the medium of cultural reproduction as well as the bearer of a white society's cultural capital, black children are confronted not only by a language that contains many words and sayings that threaten their notion of themselves but also by writings that use words, images and narratives that demean their ethnic origin and experience as well as reinforcing common stereotypes. It is not difficult, therefore, to appreciate why Patois or Creole soon assumed such importance, especially where it was necessary for intra-community communication that excluded others. The language became at once a source of pride as well as a barrier behind which the community survived. Survival had to be assured, and attempts at penetration were resisted.

Faced with such Creole speakers, British police officers were at a loss to know how to deal with individuals fluent in the language. It became impossible for them to ascertain foul language if they could not appreciate the nature of the curses or the graphic details of the swear words. To remedy this situation, the Jamaican High Commission collaborated with the police in producing a phrase book for police officers and so created the first breach in the linguistic barrier.

The resilience of the language and the determination of its speakers to maintain its exclusivity is best illustrated by the way in which popular idioms are changed once the outsider has gained access to their meanings. The outsider is invariably a figure of authority – police officer or teacher. In Patois 'to beagle' is to steal with style and panache, but once the police realized this the phrase was dropped from popular usage. Speakers turned to 'dropping sticks' to describe the same activity, with 'shelling de tek' meaning 'dividing the spoils', as one would shell peas in a pod. That too was deciphered, and change was again necessary. (It would not be expedient to reveal what is currently used, as it may already be going out of favour, just as when Richard Nixon, in concluding a speech, clenched his fist and shouted, 'Right

On!' he ensured that no self-respecting radical would ever use that phrase again.)

Excluded from society and defined as being deficient in all areas, black people have asserted their right to exist and to be defined in their own terms. Survival strategies involve the politics of confrontation as well as the cultivation of lifestyles and communal features whose characteristics and values are outside the mainstream of society. In the case of language the acquisition of competence in Creole is an expression of racial identity and solidarity as well as a demonstration of determination to acquire status and power.

Power becomes an important imperative as black people, as a result of schooling and living in the society, gain mastery over English as well as retrieving their language from the margins of society. This is a theme that has occupied several writers, most notably Daniel Defoe and William Shakespeare. Man Friday in Defoe's *Robinson Crusoe* is literature's first 'good nigger', and Caliban in Shakespeare's *The Tempest* is the first 'bad nigger'. Both are locked in a struggle with their colonial masters, who are determined to exercise domination and change them into more acceptable characters. Like colonial deities, Prospero and Robinson Crusoe can admit their black slaves to their kingdoms only if they can also communicate in the dominant tongue. Black young people today are engaged in a similar struggle. Like Caliban, they recognize the limitations of acquiring fluency in the high-status language at the expense of their own:

> You taught me language; and my profit on't
> Is, I know how to curse: the red plague rid you,
> For learning me your language!

Creole, then, is the counterbalance to this, for it gives black people the fluency not only to curse but also to acquire strength and pride.

7

The Language of Black Children and the Language Debate in Schools

JOHN RICHMOND

John Richmond's chapter on language and education faces up to the issues of racism and the politics of power described by Ansel Wong (and by Petronella Breinburg in the next chapter). As an instrument of control, schooling uses language to produce a range of success and failure in the context of social inequality. Education, the development of the individual, is another matter, but in education too language is centrally important and needs essentially to build on what is already there in the individual and the culture. This is Richmond's theme.

A preface to any statement about the language of black children must be the recognition that their language is changing. Everyone's language changes, it is true. The language of black people, particularly young black people, has changed and is changing more rapidly than that of indigenous white people because of black people's recent experience of migration, of racism and of resistance to racism. The language, and the attitude to that language, of a third-generation black British child in the 1980s will be different from the language and attitude of those who came to Britain in the 1950s. This chapter is an attempt to locate the language of black children currently in our schools in the wider debate about the teaching of language and language development, in which many teachers have now been engaged for a decade and more.

There has been substantial debate and disagreement about

what should be the response of schools to the language of black children. A number of positions have been adopted. Black children must, according to one view, abandon non-standard forms of English, at least for the purposes of education, and concentrate entirely on learning to write and speak standard English in order to maximize their chances of success in examinations, of access to post-compulsory education, of desirable and well-paid employment. This view is optimistic about social mobility; there is room at the top (or at least in the middle) for those who succeed in school, it says. It may be realistic about racism; since black children have to face prejudice and discrimination in any case, let us make as sure as we can that at least they have conventionally approved credentials. A second position proposes the same course of action for a very different purpose. Black, ethnic-minority and white working-class children must realize their common identity as a class and must learn to write and speak standard English in order not to be divided and ruled, in order to challenge inequalities of power, wealth and knowledge and eventually in order to transform society. It is interesting that two such different social intentions should produce such similar classroom intentions in this respect.

A third position asserts that our language is a crucially important part of what we are, of our history and of our culture, and that schools' ignorance of, or hostility to, languages and dialects other than standard.English is a form of oppression which must itself be challenged and transformed. Black children, it declares, will overcome the conditions of their oppression not by adopting the very language of the oppressor but by being strong and confident in their own voice. Their own voice, whatever it is, has been marginalized, caricatured, insulted, declared unfit for any reputable use. It is time that it reclaimed its authority. This position has a social intention similar to that of the second position but a quite different classroom intention.

There are other positions: for instance, a liberal humanist position, which, without radical or revolutionary social intentions, sees the right of individuals and communities to their own language and the responsibility of schools to support that right; a black separatist position, which, despairing of indiscipline or racism in state schools, seeks schools exclusively for Afro-Caribbean children and which has an approach to language arising out of a determination that separate development will provide the secure conditions in which traditional teaching methods will produce better results.

It is a complicated picture. I want to propose an attitude to the language and language development of black children that avoids ghetto-ization, that values and makes use of children's language background and competence, that recognizes the importance of written standard English. In doing this it will be necessary to make suggestions that are neither theoretically elegant nor politically pure. Nor do many of the suggestions make claim to originality. They have been said and written by other people in other places. Some of the suggestions make no specific reference to black children at all but apply in so far as those children's language, like any children's language, is affected for better or worse by the approach to its development that teachers take.

'Language' as in 'the language debate in schools', certainly means standard English or the Patois of St Lucia or Jamaican Creole, but it means a number of other things too. I think the word has at least three important meanings in the context of schools, all of which should concern us. It also has at least one improper meaning, which we should beware of.

Its improper meaning first. Over the last twenty years a very powerful attack has been mounted on two closely related ideas that were – and, despite the attack, still are – widespread in schools. These ideas are, first, that language should be taught to children in separate and graduating segments, pre-formulated and measurable; secondly, that those segments should correspond closely to grammatical parts of language, defined (normally) in terms of a grammar of English that for most linguists, has long been surpassed as a descriptive tool for the language. The attack has been informed by two powerful ideas. The first is the realization that the learning of language does not happen in separate, graduating, pre-formulated and measurable stages; language, though certainly structural, is not logical and sequential. The second powerful idea is that competence in the use of language is not the same thing as – is not even related to – having an analytical description of language. Put plainly, you do not teach children to be better writers or talkers by teaching them grammar. The grammar of a language is a very interesting area of study (to some), but it is not a prerequisite for being a good writer or talker. Grammar before or, even worse, instead of experience is the cart before the horse.

Despite this, language teaching of the cart-before-the-horse kind has shown great resistance to the attacks mounted on it. This is mainly because it is easy to do, provides great areas of security for teachers and pupils during the school week and represents, *par excellence*, the close relationship between schooling and control.

Educational publishers, incidentally, have found themselves facing in two directions about this. On the one hand, their worst fear is to be seen to be reactionary, out of date, promoting practice that has little or no intellectual justification clinging to it; on the other hand, the fact remains that there is still a big market for 'step-by-step in English', that books of this kind are quickly and cheaply written and produced and that the demand may actually have increased in the last five years. The way out of this dilemma has often been to use the word 'language', with its aura of post-Bullock enlightenment, on the covers of books whose content has not changed since the 1950s. Thus 'language' and 'language work' are offered in attractive packages that sidestep the debate, in which many teachers have been seriously engaged, about how children do actually become competent and confident users of language. That is the improper meaning of the word in the present context.

There is no order of priority to the three proper meanings I shall offer. Each of them has close connections with the others, and if we start in on one, we are quite likely to find ourselves passing through the territory of one or both of the others in the course of our investigation.

First of all, 'language' means groups of teachers sitting down together to look at the language going on in each other's classrooms. Such an activity starts from or, more likely, will pick up along the way two dimensions of under-standing, both of which include elements of dissatisfaction with schools as they are at present. The organizational dimension recognizes that schools (secondary schools in particular) must often look quite incoherent from the point of view of the pupil. Widely different teaching styles, attitudes to pupil-talk, methods of marking, approaches to reading, definitions of what constitutes valid pupil-response to teacher-questions exist side by side, hour by hour, in the pupil's week. Meanwhile, in other respects a deadening and repetitive monochrome may prevail; a pupil may be confronted with five or six passage-plus-comprehension-questions worksheets in a single day and, by the time the sixth one comes round, be utterly contemptuous of, and alienated from, school knowledge because of the way it has been presented. All this is happening at the hands of people who have, theoretically, a common aim – the education of the child. This is not, in itself, an argument for integrated studies, nor does it suggest that human variety is a bad thing and should be ironed out. It is a realization that understanding of what each is doing is likely to increase trust and respect between teachers of different subjects with different obligations and preferences, and that there are some areas – the marking of writing is one, surely – where a common decision to act in a particular way, after the problem has been discussed openly and thoroughly, must be better than the unexplained contradictions which pupils are confronted with at the moment.

The other dimension of understanding and dissatisfaction is psychological. Language and learning are crucial to each other, are totally intertwined and interpenetrating, and the more we know about how language works, the more we are likely to know about how learning happens and how to help it to happen more effectively. Unfortunately, language has often been seen as a transparent medium in which the learning is carried, and learning has been seen as lumps of knowledge which have simply to be transferred, via language, from one place to another. Once the knowledge has left the teacher's mouth, or the blackboard, it is deposited in pupils' heads or folders, where it sits until it is called for.

Put as crudely as that, it is clear that the teacher teaching is no guarantee of the learners learning. Very often we have acted as if that *were* guaranteed. One of the greatest benefits of teachers looking together at the language of each other's classrooms is that that false guarantee is challenged, and we examine more critically *interactions* within learning and get a better idea of those which are likely to produce successful and enjoyable learning and those which are not.

Secondly, 'language' has a meaning to do with the fact that schools are multi-lingual and multi-dialectal places. This has always been true, although more obviously in some places than others. Today many of our schools contain pupils who have access to a wide variety of languages and dialects. The highly prized ability to speak a foreign language, and the enormous efforts of teachers to produce individuals who can communicate in French or German, are thrown into a new light when we see 6-year-olds switching between English and an Indian language (or two), easily, appropriately, without giving much conscious thought to it; when we see 9-year-olds reading and translating into Greek, for the benefit of their grandparents, items from an English newspaper, and fifteen-year-olds who may, depending on circumstance, move between a Caribbean-French Patois, standard English, Cockney and London Jamaican. I take it as axiomatic that we should admire what children like these are capable of doing. Often in the past we have not been sufficiently admiring or supportive of their achievement. We have taken it for granted, assumed that, because such ability comes from the home or the street, it is not our business, or undervalued it because, in our eyes, the children have not had to work for it.

The only worthwhile learning, our training has told us, is arduous and difficult.

Negative judgements about what children can do with language are probably less frequent and less damning in the area of bi- or multi-lingualism than in the matter of dialect. Many teachers see it as their responsibility to encourage or force children to speak in the form associated with success as they, the teachers, perceive it, and as other powerful forces, such as employers, are said to perceive it. Given the apparent – and usually sincere – benevolence of this intention (we all want our children to do well), we become the transmitters of messages that say that, to the extent that our children's mother tongue differs from standard English pronounced in the accent of a white middle-class southerner, it is inadequate, inappropriate or incorrect. And it comes as a great shock to be told that a form or a sound that we have always thought of as wrong or rough is simply somebody else's. Engendering enormous heat in the argument, underlying it really, are the facts about class in Britain. It is very difficult for us not to make instant and persistent judgements about the quality or intelligence of a person on the basis of the way he or she speaks rather than what he or she says because class divisions and suspicions have been, and to a great extent still are, deeply rooted in British society.

Again, I take it as axiomatic that schools and teachers have a vital responsibility to value and celebrate the dialect of a child's community and culture. Deciding what the dialect is will not always be simple. Some children have access to two or three and will move between them or use mixtures of them, as a result of often unconscious decisions made in context. (Multi-lingual children use dialects too. Many of the Bengali-speaking children in London schools, for instance, speak a dialect of the language different from the Bengali of printed books.)

Those two bald statements involving the word 'axiomatic' are one prong of the dilemma. The other prong is represented by the fact that written standard English has immense power and prestige in Britain and the world today and that mass communications have seen to it that standard English is disseminated everywhere. We have a dialect of literacy, you could say. The third axiom of responsibility I would want to add to the first two is that we should help our pupils towards a fluent grasp of the dialect of literacy, of written standard English. At first glance it may seem that the two prongs of the dilemma are mutually exclusive. Surely you have to go for one or the other? I would argue not only that the two prongs are not exclusive but that they are actually complementary. Children whose language is not coterminous with standard English are more likely to be helped to write standard English in the context of information about why it is there, about why a variety of forms are available depending on who you are and where you are, than in a climate of ignorance of, or hostility to, their language. In fact, an examination of more than a century of the relationship between schooling in Britain and pupils whose vernacular speech is a non-standard dialect or a language other than English makes one thing clear: by ignoring or being hostile to language other than standard English, schools have contributed to, not alleviated, academic failure. Where are the resounding successes to be noted in schools that have operated a policy of 'Don't bring your language here'? The successes are the exceptions, not the rule.

How do we create an environment that both supports children's vernacular and recognizes the importance of written standard English?

We should not try to standardize children's speech. It very probably will not work, and it will certainly be taken by children, however nicely we put it, as a negative judgement on themselves. People do change their speech because of perceptions they have about what is socially acceptable or economically desirable, it is true; if that change is going to happen, then they must be the authors of it themselves. Teachers will certainly do a lot more harm than good by trying to enforce it.

Those children who have access to, and want to use, a non-standard form of the language as a conscious part of their work should be encouraged to do so and made to feel the possessors of an enviable ability rather than the inheritors of a linguistic defect. Narrative writing, poetry, playwriting and drama provide the most obvious opportunities for this.

In the primary school and the early years of secondary school we should not attempt to standardize the (usually very small) number of non-standard features that intervene unconsciously in some children's mainstream school writing. The damage done to children's confidence and fluency as writers by the early and sometimes constant rejection of their language is considerable. And there is plenty to work on in helping children to develop their writing in areas not related to dialect. That statement, of course, assumes that teachers know the difference between a non-standard feature and a conventional error in the first place. A non-standard feature is not necessarily a straightforward case of the intervention of non-standard grammar, though it may often be that. It may also be a transitional form that is used in the process of acquiring control of written standard language.

At some point in the middle years of secondary school, if it is obvious that some pupils are continuing to produce non-standard features in their writing for which they will ultimately be penalized, teachers should point out to them what those features are, and what their standard equivalents are. At what point? The hardest question. The difficulty with any attempt to say 'now' is that it ignores the fact that learners mature at different rates, are capable of acts of objectivity at different times. I have met 12-year-olds ready and anxious to talk about dialect differences and 15-year-olds who did not perceive differences as differences when I pointed them out. So the decision about exact timing, as so often, must rest with the teacher, whose intuition and knowledge of the learner's development is likely to be shrewder than a blanket statement got from a book. The one point worth repeating is that it must not be forced too early. It is just as brutal, and eventually counterproductive, to inflict conformity to standard

English on younger children, consciously, in the name of the appropriate, as to inflict it ignorantly in the name of the correct.

It is worth saying, since this is a knot of the argument that habitually detains people and assumes a very large significance, that what we are doing nearly all the time is not teaching standard English as standard English but teaching English as English, and that by far the most important task for us is to decide what we need to know and do in order to foster writers who are competent and confident, and who see themselves *as* writers, whatever their linguistic background.

A valuable way of linking positively the great variety of linguistic competence in our classrooms with the importance of written standard English forms is the third proper meaning of 'language', and it takes us back to the argument about language learned through experience or through separate and graduating abstract segments presented in drills and exercises. One of the most frequently heard voices in this argument has been the voice that says, 'All right, I take the point. I'm fed up with those old drills and exercises anyway. But what do I do instead?' That is an absolutely legitimate worry. You have been teaching in a certain way, using certain books and materials, because you thought that was your job and because those books and materials were there in the stock cupboard. It has been fairly dull, but at least the children have been engaged in something and some of them actually seem to enjoy it. Now this clever individual tells you it is all a waste of time. What is the alternative?

One good alternative is the study of language itself, which is currently an increasingly important dimension of the teaching of English. It can lead to work that is more varied, more enlightened, more fun, involving children in more interaction, more reflection on their own experience, and offers them extensions of and parallels to that experience, which has historical, geographical and sociological angles to it. It can provoke activities where children talk, write, listen, read, tape, role-play, analyse, think, work individually, in pairs, in groups, as a whole class or in combinations of those four.

Quality and control in children's writing can, and should be, discussed using the writing the children actually produce (which holds true, of course, throughout the curriculum).

I am selling it very hard here, I know. It sounds optimistic as it stands. There are dangers and disadvantages. I have mentioned publishers' spurious imitations: nice glossy cover, multi-cultural scene, title *Looking at Language Now*, chapter one 'Nouns'. If children are pacified by books of this kind, if we can actually walk into a room, hand out a set and get them to do the exercises on page 42, finished off for homework, they may well object to the inconvenience of being asked to think about something for a change, read more extensively, write more continuously, discuss something together. Life may become more difficult for a while. Another danger to avoid: we are not attempting to turn children into mini-linguists. Lectures from the front on discourse analysis or West African Creoles will not receive more attention than we would be entitled automatically to expect of lectures from the front about anything else. That is, teacher talking to the class is one, only one, of the methods by which children learn. And there are people around at the moment who want to claim for linguistics an authority which would take us straight back to transmission teaching in new clothes. 'Get your language model right,' they say, 'and go in there and teach it. It was just that we had an inadequate description of language before.' The old description, inherited from the public schools in the late nineteenth century (they themselves having inappropriately borrowed it from the study of classical languages), was certainly inadequate. If, however, we abandon what we know about the need for learners to be active, about the range of contexts in which they learn, about collaboration and talk, about the way learners' bring their own experience to the learning process, in favour of an authoritarian pedagogy with the gilt edge of new linguistics, we shall be no further forward – in fact, a good deal further back.

Assuming that we can avoid that trap, the study of language offers us a way of giving our pupils reasons for the celebration of variety in language *and* a more objective awareness of dialect differences, a way of helping them to feel proud of their natural speech *and* enthusiastic about becoming literate in standard English. It offers us a chance to investigate together, among other things, why languages and dialects exist, the wealth of languages in the world and the connections between them, how people came to write, how English has emerged, the rise of standard English, the connection between language and class, the effect of the mass media on attitudes to language, matters like style and register, the reasons why English is now a world language, the language of the street or the playground, jokes, rhymes, games, the whole oral culture – and, in the course of doing this, to introduce our pupils to literature that represents the multi-dialectal nature of English and to show something of the role of literature in other languages and cultures.

I want to finish by returning to our first proper meaning of 'language'. What I called there 'groups of teachers sitting down together to look at the language going on in each other's classrooms' is, of course, the grass-roots form of language across the curriculum. That phrase, at its best, means teachers and schools asking themselves critical questions in a spirit of trust and deciding to act coherently, though not necessarily uniformly, as a result. All the topics I have mentioned, whether they have specific relevance to black children or whether they are concerned with all children as learners, should be part of the matter on which a language policy that means something to the lives of learners and teachers might be based.

If black people's language has changed over the last two generations in Britain, it is certain that the change will continue in the future. How the language of black children in British schools in the early part of the next century will be regarded, whether or not it will be seen as 'an issue', is impossible to predict. It may be that other realities, such as the long-term unemployment of young black people, will dwarf the significance of discussions like this. Teachers in schools, meanwhile, must hold on to certain principles in their sphere of influence and must not capitulate to the reductionist functionalism that characterizes the educational and political mood at the moment. Black children's language has a history, has variety, has power. We must help them to know that history, to exercise choice over that variety, to realize that power.

8

Language Attitudes:
the Case of Caribbean Language

PETRONELLA BREINBURG

In this chapter Petronella Breinburg deals with the social psycho-logy of language attitudes and 'person perception', and the interac-tion between the two. Language alters society and vice versa. The process has an important effect on education. We suggest that the difficult task of sorting prejudice from informed opinion, objectify-ing it and so (hopefully) reducing or eliminating it, should be undertaken by teachers and lecturers, whether they have black students or not. As Petronella Breinburg points out, academics are not untouched by these prejudices.

We have had the 'Deficit Theory' (Bernstein, 1971) and we have had the 'Difference Theory' (Labov, 1972) to explain why working-class children under-achieve in Britain's educa-tion system. Now blacks, sometimes called Afro-Caribbeans or West Indians or Black British, have taken over from the working class. It is no longer the working-class child who suffers from the 'deficit' or 'difference', but the 'black' child of negroid race. But neither the 'deficit' nor the 'difference' school pays enough attention to the fact that it may be neither deficit nor difference that is the real issue, but *who* it is whose language is responded to.

To illustrate, this chapter commences with two brief stor-ies, which are similar to recurring dreams because they keep emerging in one form or another.

The first story is set at a linguistic conference in Belgium in August 1984. A Dutch scholar made the statement that, as far as he was concerned, Afrikaans is Creole-Dutch. He was supported by another (Stoops, forthcoming), who gave a list of sentences to illustrate the Creole-Portuguese influence on the structure of Afrikaans, among them the following:

Dutch: *Ik heb hem gezien.* (I have seen him.)
          I have him saw.

Afrikaans: *Ek heb vir hem gezien.* (I have seen him.)
          I have for him saw.

The significant indicator is the lexical item *vir* (*voor* in Dutch).

The question then raised in connection with this paper was, 'If Afrikaans is evidently a Creole-Dutch, why is it considered a language, while Caribbean Creoles, which are Creolized English, Creolized Portuguese or Creolized French, are called *dialects* of the parent language?'

The argument became political, and no linguistic reason was given. The point was made, however, that we cannot compare the language of a highly developed nation (e.g. the Afrikaners) with that of an under-developed nation. Also Afrikaans is a written language.

The second story is set in France in August 1984. A British teacher of further education showed great pleasure when she reported that she had heard a young man speaking and realized that he was black only when she turned around: 'Isn't that nice? He speaks just like us [whites].' When eventually the young man was spoken to in connection with this paper, it emerged that he spoke Cockney; in fact, listening to him was like listening to a white stall-holder selling his wares in Bethnal Green Street market, in the heart of Cockney-land. Praise for non-standard white dialect when used by black children in Britain, yet the condemnation of Creole, is as common as the acceptance of Afrikaans as a language but the rejection of Caribbean Creoles, especially Jamaican Creole (which must not be confused with Jamaican English, since the two are completely different (Bailey, 1966).

Non-standard white dialect, spoken by working-class whites, is what deficit theorists such as Bernstein first emphasized until blacks and their language became the issue. Yet teachers and some black parents continue to praise this dialect when spoken by black people of Caribbean origin and condemn Creoles, whether the Caribbean or the British varieties. The question is: Why?

To answer this question it was necessary to carry out a study through an interdisciplinary approach, relying heavily on what Giles and St Clair (1979) refer to as the symbiotic relationship between sociolinguistics and social psychology.

The Theory

In order to explore the possibly significant relationship between perception and response to language we must be clear about what sort of perception we are considering, what the basic tenets of that kind of perception are and how they may relate to response to language variation.

Person perception, sometimes referred to as social perception, is a special category of perception (Cantril, 1968). Person or social perception refers to the processes by which we come to think about other persons, their characteristics, qualities and inner states (Taguiri, 1969). We perceive people and interpret their speech by means of cues based on our theories. These theories then determine our predictions. For example, a group of teachers in London and one in Amsterdam made similar predictions when they were given a series of writings to read. They were told that these writings were from a multi-cultural school. Teachers at once predicted, perhaps subconsciously, that there would be Creole interference and hence found 'evidence' of such interference. The truth of the matter was that all the children were white, and not one was from a Creole-speaking background or had any close contact with Creole speakers. Two conclusions emerge: one is that the teachers' prediction was made based on theory, previously formulated; the second is that it was *inaccurate*. The issue of inaccuracy is the most problematic in perception. Often we 'see' what is not there at all. This 'binocular disparity' (as it has been referred to by Brunswik, 1956) is often based on insufficient evidence or verbal hearsay (Vernon, 1963).

Another important aspect of person perception is that we perceive people in groups. As Bannister and Fransella (1971) have pointed out, if we see a man who is black, we attribute to him all the characteristics and traits we mentally associate with black people. This mental association in turn influences our predictions and our response to that person (Bender and Hastorf, 1950). Another aspect of group perception – that is, how one group of people views another – is that people belonging to the same culture or ethnic group view both the world around them and other groups of people in a similar (though not necessarily identical) manner. Kelly (1955) draws attention to this culture-group perception under his 'commonality corollary'.

But how does all of this relate to response to language? Giles and St Clair (1979) draw attention to the dynamics of self-perception and the perception of others and how these may be related to the way in which we perceive the language of other people. They carried out a number of experiments and observations, using mainly the match-guise technique and concentrating primarily on the phonological aspect of language. They found, for example, that response to speech is influenced by the identity, or supposed identity, of the speaker. In his Canadian study Giles used a perfect bilingual speaker (someone who was fully competent in, and equally familiar with, two languages). He observed that when the speaker changed from French to English the judges' response to him changed from negative to positive but only because they were not aware that it was the same person speaking on both occasions.

In my own study I looked at language and dialect variety in general, incorporating both spoken and written language. I sought to test the hypothesis that there appears to be a relationship between person perception (*PP*) and perception of (hence response to) language (*LP*). In other words, my study set out to find the value of *r*, as shown in the figure below, where *r* is the relationship between *PP* and *LP*:

$$PP \leftarrow r \rightarrow LP$$

The Method

I used a multi-method to collect the data. The approach I adopted followed along a continuum, starting with a totally uncontrolled observation and proceeding to systematic questioning, followed by semi-structured interviews and four case studies, then finally to a structured small-scale survey using interview schedules. The study took place first of all in London, travelled to Amsterdam for a Dutch/British comparison and is now continuing in Sheffield. In this chapter I shall base my argument on the London study.

I chose ten schools, one each from the ten Inner London Education Authorities, through random sampling. From these, I selected three schools, again at random. Within each of these three schools 20 per cent of the total teaching staff was chosen at random, giving me a total of forty-two teachers. Because these teachers were selected at random, as were the schools, I argue that they represent a fair cross-section of the teachers in Inner London schools.

I then prepared an interview schedule. The items on the schedule were selected from statements made by teachers, community educators and lecturers involved in teachers' education. A five-point Likert (1967) scale, ranging from 'very much agree' to 'very much disagree', was employed. Those who did not know or wished to remain neutral had the opportunity to tick number 3. Those who did not reply to a specific statement were given -1 for that statement.

To analyse the data I used a modified version of Kelly's repertory grid technique employing factor analysis, with a Pearson correlation – but the data has since been put through several other tests. A Statistic Package for the Social Sciences (SPSS) was used.

Results

To find out first of all if there was a close correlation between person perception and language perception I subjected all of the data to a Pearson's correlation test, through SPSS. The result, which can be seen below, is that there appears to be a very close correlation, since $r = 0.8051$ and the probability (P) of this result being by chance is very low (42 being the number of teachers):

	LP
	0.8051
PP	(42)
	$p = 0.001$

But correlation does not give us causation, so the data was further tested through what SPSS refers to as a 'one-way' analysis. Language perception was taken to be the depending factor (it depends on person perception) and person perception the independent one (it does not depend on language perception). Again a close correlation, with a low probability, emerged. But when person perception was taken as the depending factor (depending on language perception) there appeared to be a statistically insignificant correlation.

Another interesting factor emerged when the large grid obtained (the square on which all thirty-two questions were set against the forty-two teachers' answers) was studied closely. There appeared to be evidence that individual teachers' scores on the language perception statement matched that of the person perception statement. There were very few cases (a negligible number) in which there was a slight difference between the two types of score.

For further scrutiny a SPSS programme using a 'one-way' analysis of variance for specific variables was used. (Person perception was kept constant, while language perception, the other factor, was changed.) A statistic measure of means and standard deviations was also taken. See Table 1.

Table 1   A matrix for language perception as a dependent factor of the person/language perception relationship after a 'one-tailed' directional study

Items	Mean	Standard deviation	F-ratio	F-probability (p)
1	2.9	1.4	9.750	$p < 0.003$
2	3.0	1.4	10.571	$p < 0.002$
3	3.0	1.3	5.167	$p < 0.024$
4	3.4	1.1	3.818	$p < 0.052$
5	3.5	1.4	0.284	$p < 0.757$
6	2.9	1.4	2.076	$p < 0.168$
7	3.0	1.4	3.523	$p < 0.062$
8	3.3	1.1	0.415	$p < 0.669$

In the table we note that from a 'one-tailed' directional study in which we took language perception as the dependent factor, there appears to be strong evidence that, as we found after our Pearson's correlation test, language perception is closely correlated with person perception. There is no evidence of causality. The table does not indicate whether there are other factors which may have acted on language perception but not on person perception. Until such factors are adduced as evidence we can infer from the table that language perception is a factor depending on person perception or on that plus other factors.

It is justifiable to take person perception as a whole because a factor analysis, as stated before and in Breinburg (1984a), shows that there is a high correlation between the items on the person perception list. By this I mean that the same percentage (or near enough) of teachers who construe that blacks suffer from an inferiority complex also construe blacks as aggressive and so on. When we take the inter-group correlation and the means square, again we get a high correlation, with the probability of the findings being by chance very low.

We can now examine the data to see if the same teachers

who have a negative person perception also have a negative attitude to language perception. Recall that a score of 5 points means 'very much disagree' while a score of 1 point means 'very much agree'. If, for instance, the teacher who disagrees that black people have an inferiority complex also disagrees that Creole has no place in school, then this is a further indication that there appears to be a close correlation between responses (positive in this case) to person perception and to language perception.

We shall now take a sample from the larger matrix. Table 2 represents an extract from the larger grid (42 × 16).

Table 2   A matrix showing the person/language relationship, where the cases (teachers) are 1–42, language perception = 1–8, person perception = 9–16, scale is 1–5. The three main items on the language perception and on the person perception list are taken. 'No reply' is coded −1.

Case		*Language perception items*			*Person perception items*		
no.		1	2	3	9	10	11
(a)	2	5	5	5	5	5	5
	22	4	4	4	4	4	4
	25	5	5	5	5	5	5
	26	4	4	4	4	4	4
(b)	21	1	1	1	1	1	1
	34	2	2	2	2	2	2
	38	2	2	2	2	2	2
(c)	4	2	2	2	2	−1	3
	7	5	5	5	3	4	5
	12	−1	5	5	1	−1	−1
	13	1	1	1	1	5	3

In the table we have some positive responses, 'very much disagree' and 'disagree' (a); these are followed by negative responses, 'very much agree' and 'agree' (b). We note that the teachers who reply positively and say that they very much disagree or disagree that blacks have an inferiority complex also disagree or very much disagree that Creole is a handicap or has no place in school. The argument here is not whether the teacher is correct in saying that Creole is not a handicap or that blacks do not suffer from an inferiority complex. The issue is how teachers' scores show a relationship between person perception and language perception. At (c) the relationship is not so straightforward because we note slight differences between the scores on language perception and people perception – for instance, at teacher 4. The greatest differences are those of teacher 12, who has three 'no reply' and two 'very much disagree'. The correlation between person and language perception does not appear to be close.

The Three Schools Compared

The most interesting result appeared when the three schools were compared. The school with the lowest percentage of black children gave the most negative response. In this school most of the teachers either 'very much agree' or 'agree' that blacks have an inferiority complex and lack self-confidence, and that they have an inferior education, and also 'very much agree' or 'agree' that blacks have a language problem, that they have a limited vocabulary, that Creole is a handicap, that black dialect has no place in school and so on.

If we look at the total of the three schools, we note the difference between schools X, Y and Z on the eight language perception (1–8) and eight person perception (9–16) statements, which can be seen below. Table 3 is a summary of the results of the test carried out to compare the schools. The table concerns itself with the 'core item' on the language perception list (i.e. item 1, 'Blacks have more of a language problem than do whites'), against the whole person perception (PP) list, in the 'one-tailed' analysis and a T-test.

Table 3 shows, first of all, that none of the results occurred by chance. We also note that there is a significant difference (3.100) between the F-ratio of schools X and Y. In addition we recall that school X had over 50 per cent black children, while school Y had about 15 per cent. We can infer that the

Table 3 Difference between means of three schools (SCL) on the dependent item list (construct types) taking the 'core item' (1) on the list against all the items on the PP (independent) list

Item 1	F-ratio	F-probability (p)
SCL X	6.650	$p < 0.014$
SCL Y	7.899	$p < 0.005$
SCL Z	9.750	$p < 0.003$

lower percentage of black children produced a higher score when item 1 is correlated with person perception. When we look at school Z (just over 1 per cent black children) we note a reinforcement to the argument just presented because school Y, though producing a higher F-ratio and hence a more significant relationship between item 1 and person perception than did school X, this is not so in the case of school Z. We note that it is school Z that produced the highest score if we consider the F-ratio from lowest (6.650) to highest (9.750). We note that the theory that a higher percentage of black children affects teachers' constructs of blacks as people and their language appears to be borne out. We can safely say that from the results of this test, summarized above, it would appear that teachers' constructs and responses do not appear to be based on knowledge or facts about the group they are construing – that is, if we take it that teachers' knowledge is based on their personal contact with black children. Teachers may obtain their information from other sources, however, including the mass media, from which they may develop a stereotyped view. Here we see how difficult an area this is. We can argue only from the results before us. We cannot discuss whether teachers' constructs are based on knowledge or not: we have no evidence to support either contention. We can say only that the number of black children in a school does not appear to affect teachers' construing of blacks as having more language problems, which is the core of the whole language perception construct argument, which in turn seems to be dependent on how teachers construe blacks as a group of people.

Summary and Conclusions

We note that there appears to be strong evidence that the response to language of a group of people is closely correlated with perception. Attitude to language can be studied within the area of sociolinguistics, while social perception is specifically a social-psychological phenomenon. It follows, then, that a combination of sociolinguistics and social psychology theory and methodology can be of great value in the study of language in a setting as complex as that of the response to the language of black people within a white/black conflict situation.

In this study teachers' perception of black children of Caribbean background appears generally to be what this study regards as negative and stereotyped, and this finding significantly correlates with the response to the mother tongue and speech patterns of black people of Caribbean origin.

No doubt there are limitations to a small-scale, one-person study with restricted resources. Further study will have to be carried out. But from the information gathered so far, especially a qualitative study that shows that change in language (a linguistic shift) does not correspond with change in person perception, while change in person perception corresponds to change in response to language, it seems that there is reason to believe that person perception influences language perception, as we saw from the 'one-way' analysis. In this analysis the latter was dependent on the former, still showing a very close correlation with a very low probability. This suggests that linguistic arguments which exclude social psychology are not getting to the roots of the problem.

If, as this study suggests, it is the way in which teachers perceive black children of Caribbean background that is the issue, then surely both the 'deficit' and the 'difference' theorists have to begin to turn their attention to perception, hence to social psychology. Such theorists and others who carry out research into language and educational attainment should now begin to address themselves more to the issue of perception and less to purely linguistic features. Until this issue receives closer attention, the argument of whether or not the Black West Indian has a linguistic deficit or difference will continue. I suggest that more detailed comparative studies of the relationship, for instance, between Afrikaans and Dutch and between Caribbean Creole and British English would also be of great help, for they would assist both the 'difference' and the 'deficit' schools in answering the question of why Afrikaans is called a 'language' but Jamaican Creole a 'dialect' or a debased form of English. Once that question is answered the reason for the present response to the language of children of Caribbean origin will become somewhat clearer. And once the *reason* for a phenomenon is known, steps can be taken towards a cure, if this is desired.

One can argue, of course, that there may not be a desire to cure a disease, or change an attitude, even if the cause is known. It can be that there is no wish to change the present negative attitude to the language or speech patterns of certain people. It can also be that teachers and those involved in education feel much more at ease if the educational 'underachievement' (so-called) of the children of West Indian background can be explained through language. No doubt it is better to say now that 'language' is the problem rather than to return to the old explanation of the 'low intelligence' of the black race or social and home background factors.

The question of racial factors and the West Indian child has now been flogged to death. The issue is much more than just race. Many West Indians are of Asian or European background. Their speech patterns are not included when many teachers and linguists talk about a 'black dialect' or 'black English'. Many West Indians are of the same negroid race as many Africans, yet the language or speech patterns of the Africans are more acceptable to the dominant group than are those of the West Indians of the same race.

Even the term 'stereotype' (and our concept of it) has been overworked. Stereotyped attitudes have existed, still exist and will, predictably, continue to exist in Britain and elsewhere. This prediction is based on the finding of my longitudinal study of the relationship between perception and response to language over the course of five years. The stereotyped view of certain groups of people that existed at the beginning was exactly the same at the end of the five years and still exists now that the project has moved on another two years. And this is in spite of race awareness and in-service courses around England attended by many of the respondents to the study.

I hope that a study of this kind, though it will not change attitudes, will bring to attention the fallacy that it is a question of deficit or difference between languages that is at issue.

9

London Jamaican and Black London English

MARK SEBBA

Can London Jamaican – the English-based Creole of black Londoners – be said to exist as a stable language? Its psychological and
cultural reality are unquestionable. Mark Sebba shows that many
speakers pass through – some never supersede – an apprenticeship
during which Creole rules are applied (inconsistently) to an English
'base'. Paradoxically, their version of London English shows a few
far-reaching, Creole-derived features. And the whole opens up
creative possibilities for its speakers. Significantly, Sebba does not
view this range as a continuum, a concept now questioned by
several linguists in the Caribbean too. Support also comes from
Edwards's and Sutcliffe's research in the West Midlands (1985)
suggesting that a majority of young black people there are perfect
or near-perfect bilinguals.

> Denise and Cheryl was yaso.
> *Graffito in Southern Region train, 1984*

In the thirty years or so since the London Afro-Caribbean
community began to establish itself a number of interesting
linguistic events have taken place.* First, the first-generation

* The research on which this chapter is based was supported by a small grant from
the Nuffield Foundation and a project grant (No. HR 8682) from the Economic and
Social Research Council. I am grateful to R. B. Le Page and D. Sutcliffe for
comments on this chapter. They are not, of course, responsible for any of its
shortcomings. I would also like to record my appreciation of all the help I have
received from my many informants and those who have helped me to get in touch
with them.

migrants from the West Indies found themselves living and working among speakers of 'London English' – Cockney, as it is often called – a variety that was probably unfamiliar to nearly all of them. Many of them adapted their speech to this variety in different ways, depending on their degree of exposure to it and on other factors.

In 1961 and 1962 the British Government passed two Commonwealth Immigrants Acts. From then on, for economic as well as political reasons, the number of migrants coming from the West Indies to Britain has declined almost to nothing. The result is that a majority of those under twenty-four years old, and thus a large proportion of the younger generation, were actually born in London and have grown up there. Among this group – natives of London but with strong family and cultural links with the Caribbean – not one but at least two and perhaps more indigenous language varieties have arisen. One of these is a local form of Jamaican Creole, which has come to be called by linguists 'London Jamaican', though it is called 'Jamaican', 'dialect', 'Patois', 'black talk' or 'bad English' by most of its speakers, who are not all of Jamaican descent. The other variety that I shall discuss I call Afro-Caribbean London English. It is the local London English (Cockney) spoken conversationally by black Londoners and is different, in a few small but interesting respects, from the London English spoken by other local people in the same area.

In this chapter I will describe the two varieties, Afro-Caribbean London English and London Jamaican, and will try to give an account of how they are used by young members of the Afro-Caribbean community in London. This is not an insider account, although many of the recordings on which it is based were made by members of that community among their families and friends. The analysis itself is the work of an outsider and so necessarily lacks some of the insights that a member of the community might have. I hope that in the near future an insider will come forward to study these phenomena. His or her conclusions may well differ from mine. In the meantime, these are my findings.

Afro-Caribbean London English

In contrast to their parents, who are native speakers of various types of Caribbean Creole (Jamaican, Grenadian, Barbadian, Trinidadian, Guyanese, Vincentian, St Lucian, Montserrat, etc.) or of a West Indian variety of Standard English, or of two or more of these, the young black people of London, with few exceptions, are native speakers of London English – the type of English sometimes called Cockney, though this term has a more specific meaning for some people. In addition they are likely to be able to speak London Jamaican, and some of them can also speak the Caribbean Creole of one or other of their parents. However, most of them are, first and foremost, speakers of London English. Among women nearly all conversation seems to be carried on in London English except in certain, reasonably well defined, circumstances, when Creole is used. Among males the situation is different, although my data are based on too limited a range of encounters for me to draw any firm conclusions. In formal situations, such as at school and when white people are present, London English is likely to be used. In more relaxed encounters and when white people are not present London Jamaican will probably be used at least some of the time. On the whole, London English seems to be used in a wider range of circumstances by women than by men, though women can speak London Jamaican as fluently as men, and sometimes more so. It may be the case, though, that men tend to speak a 'deeper' variety of London Jamaican – that is, a variety more different from London English and closer to Jamaican Creole.

I have said that the London English used by Afro-Caribbeans is slightly different from that of their white neighbours. The differences are quite small, and many of them would probably go unnoticed except by a linguist. They are interesting partly because the acquisition of the local language by the Afro-Caribbean community is so complete – in contrast to the local English culture, which many of the younger generation reject – that these small tokens of a Caribbean linguistic connection are potentially important social markers.

All the differences between Afro-Caribbean London English and 'ordinary' London English that I have found seem to be due to influence from Jamaican Creole or, possibly, other Caribbean Creoles. Afro-Caribbean London English differs from white London English at the syntactic, lexical and phonetic levels, as discussed below.

Phonetic and Prosodic Features

It seems to be true – as it is an experience that I have had many times and share with many others – that something in the tone of voice of black Londoners gives a clue to their ethnicity, so that a hearer can sometimes guess that they are black without having seen them. Since the various socio-economic and geographical varieties of London English and their phonetic characteristics have not been well studied, one can hardly do more than guess at what exactly are the salient distinguishing features of black London speech. One possibility is that the norms for pitch, rhythm, volume, vowel length, nasality, aspiration, breathiness, etc., or some combination of these, are slightly different for black speakers. Although the differences may be small, together they may add up to a 'black accent'. Another possible source of the different 'sound' of black speech is that different norms of use may apply to the various alternative realizations of certain phonemes, e.g. [f] *versus* [θ] for orthographic *th* in *thing*. The [f] pronunciation, which is part of the Cockney stereotype, seems to be in more frequent use among young blacks than among whites in the same age group, making it part of the 'black stereotype' too (compare Sutcliffe, 1982, for a similar finding on black English in Bedford). In fact, it is well established in London Jamaican, where it has replaced the initial [t] in *truu* ('through') for some speakers. If the [f] pronunciation of *th* is really on the increase among black speakers and declining among white speakers – and no research has actually been done on this – this would suggest that in the black community the norms for the use of such social markers are different from those in the white community and may, in fact, be more conservative norms, which the more upwardly mobile white working class has already discarded. This remains to be investigated.

Lexis

In a community in which code-switching is as central to linguistic behaviour as it is among the Afro-Caribbean community in London (see below), the problem necessarily arises of deciding whether a word of West Indian origin embedded in an otherwise London English environment is an instance of code-switching or has been 'borrowed' or 'naturalized' into black London English. The only reasonably reliable criterion for deciding this is a phonetic one: is there an observable deviation from any of the phonetic parameters associated with London English that lasts for just the duration of that word? If the answer is yes, then we are probably dealing with a code-switch. If no, then the lexical item is apparently being used as if it were just another London English word. The number of West Indian words used in this way is not very large, and there may be considerable variation from speaker to speaker. Some examples I have recorded are *hug up* ('hug, cuddle' – *up* is an intensifier), *picky-picky* ('peppercorn hair' but, in this case, referring to some synthetic cloth), *duppy* ('ghost'), *facety* ('impertinent'). It is reasonable to assume that only the first of these would be understood by a speaker from outside the Afro-Caribbean community without some explanation.

The word *stay*, when it is a pseudo copula functioning as a substitute for an adjectival verb, as in *you know how people stay* ('you know what people are like'), could be an instance of either lexical or syntactic influence from a Caribbean language variety.

Syntax and Morphology

Black speakers have a strong tendency to use a word pronounced like London English *say*, though sometimes with a

shorter vowel or lacking the second element of the diphthong, following a verb of knowing, believing, perceiving,
etc., where London English would have *that*. This element
[sɛ] or [sɛɪ] clearly is related to the Jamaican Creole item *se*
(cf. entry on *se* in Cassidy and Le Page 1980:396): 'After
verbs such as *think*, *know*, *believe*, *suppose*, *see*, or others
involving communications, as *tell*, *hear*, *promise*, introducing
the object clause: virtually equivalent to *that*. (Sometimes
that is used redundantly after it.)'

As might be expected, this *se* is a regular feature of London
Jamaican, reflecting its close relation to Jamaican Creole.
However, it also occurs regularly in the speech of young
black people when they are speaking London English. I have
examples on tape from different speakers in widely separated
parts of London. Here are some of them:

Example 1
(a) If we lose, we lose, we know *se* we tried (female, aged 16)
(b) A all white jury found out *se* 'e was guilty (male, aged 15)
(c) Sometimes fings 'appen, right [*pause*] and you know *se*
    really an' truly it ain't gonna work out (female, aged 20)
(d) I feel *se* they're 'olding it over there you know (female,
    aged 15)

The incorporation of an item like this into the grammar of
London English represents quite an important change. It is
not merely a lexical substitution of *se* for *that*, for two
reasons: first, the people who use *se* also have at least a
passive knowledge of *that* used in the same positions by non-
black speakers. Secondly, *se* replaces *that* only in certain
contexts, namely after a verb of knowing, believing, etc., and
not in expressions like *the fact that*, *that I'm tired is not
surprising*, etc., where *se* could not occur in Creole either.
This means that the introduction of *se* into London English
has actually involved a restructuring of the complementizer
system to include a new element, and possibly changes in the
lexicon as well, since a class of verbs must be marked out as
being followed by *se*. This would make the grammar of these

speakers' London English similar to the grammar of Jamaican Creole in this respect, potentially a rather far-reaching change. It is puzzling that this particular construction should have been selected for incorporation into London English. Although, strictly speaking, *se* is redundant in the contexts where it occurs (in the sense that it does not affect meaning), it must provide some opportunity for confusion and misunderstandings between black and white speakers. But black speakers do not suppress *se* when speaking to whites: examples 1(a) and (b) were said to me and in relatively formal contexts. The conclusion is that speakers are not aware of it, unless they are using it deliberately to distance themselves in a rather subtle way. If *se* persists (instead of dying out under pressure from 'proper' English), it may become part of a stereotype of black London speech. For more on *se* and its African origins, see Sebba (1984a).

I have tried to show that the London English of black native speakers is different in fairly small but potentially important respects from the London English of other communities. What I have not been able to do – because no research has been done on this topic – is to show whether, or how, the distinctly black variety of London English is regarded as a special, community-based variety either by blacks themselves or by others. It seems likely that at the moment most of the characteristics that distinguish Afro-Caribbean London English from other types of London English are below the level of conscious awareness of speakers in the black community and in other communities. Whether this will continue to be the case depends on social, political, historical and linguistic factors – among them the fate of London Jamaican, which I shall discuss in the next section.

London Jamaican

The degree of acquaintance that young London-born blacks have with their parents' native language varieties varies greatly. It often is the case that the parents themselves (some of whom have been in Britain for thirty years) considerably modify their language in the direction of London English, so that their children do not hear Creole spoken at home except in a rather anglicized form. I have found that some Afro-Caribbean children look on Creole speech as an object of fun or derision. Some claim not to be able to speak it, although this claim should not usually be taken at face value. There are several possible reasons for this attitude, but the most important is probably the low esteem in which Creole languages are held by the parents themselves (an attitude that they would most likely have brought with them from the West Indies) and the negative attitude to, and misunderstanding of, non-standard varieties of language that still prevails in many schools. Alternatively, it may be part of a general rejection of the behaviour of the older generation.

In contrast, the variety of speech that has come to be called London Jamaican is widely spoken by the younger generation of blacks, especially males, and there is considerable peer-group pressure to learn to speak it. It is clear that this language variety is not learned solely from adults in the home. First, there are many reports (e.g. in Sutcliffe, 1982) that adults disapprove of the use of this variety in the home. Although this is certainly not true in every case, and may in fact be true only in a minority of homes, it does seem that the use of London Jamaican by children is tolerated rather than encouraged. Secondly, the relatedness of London Jamaican and Jamaican Creole is obvious. Although the two are different, London Jamaican must be regarded as a variety of Jamaican and not of Barbadian, Trinidadian, Guyanese, etc. However, London Jamaican is spoken by children from homes where none of the adults is from a Jamaican background, as well as from homes where the adults have Jamaican links. (Though Jamaicans were by far the largest group of migrants to London, there are significant communities of people from most of the other Caribbean countries. Many children have grown up in homes where the adults come from two or more of these countries.)

Thirdly, although a large number of London Jamaican speakers *do* come from homes where there are Jamaican

adults, the Creole speech of these adults is sufficiently different from London Jamaican for the two varieties to be
regarded as distinct in their origins. A London-born black
person in Jamaica can be identified as a 'foreigner' by speech
as well as by other clues. Fourthly, London Jamaican is to a
large extent an adolescent and post-adolescent phenomenon.
My research suggests that pre-adolescents have relatively
little interest in it, but as they grow older they become more
and more inclined to use it. It is primarily the language of the
youth culture associated with reggae, Rastafari and 'sounds'.
As this culture has itself spread outward and attracted many
people from outside the black community, so the language,
London Jamaican, has been acquired by white as well as
black adolescents (see Hewitt, 1982).

Although I have referred to London Jamaican as a language, it is not a language in quite the same sense as, say,
Jamaican Creole. This is because London Jamaican is
acquired mainly in adolescence, from the peer group, by
individuals whose first language is normally (black) London
English. While London Jamaican speakers may aim to produce speech that is maximally 'deep' (or 'bad'), meaning as
close as possible to Jamaican Creole, most of the time they do
not do this. This is partly because of a tendency to code-
switch between London Jamaican and London English (see
below), which has the effect of 'diluting' the Jamaican element. However, it also seems to be because for many of its
speakers London Jamaican is not a separate language but a
system of adaptations, each with stereotypical value, which is
applied to London English. Which of these adaptations is
applied, and where, depends on the individual speaker and
the particular speech act, and there is the possibility of a
trade-off relation between some of the elements in the system,
so that using one feature which is strongly marked as 'Jamaican' may make it unnecessary to use another feature.

An illustration may make this clearer. It is worth pointing
out that, in my view, research conducted on London Jamaican that does not use conversational data is self-defeating.
This is because the use of the two codes London English and

London Jamaican (and perhaps others, though this would take us too far afield) is itself a conversational strategy, and it is not possible (again, in my opinion) to account adequately for the use of London Jamaican and the particular features of London Jamaican that are used, except in a conversational context. So in the following extract the speech of both participants is given. Pauses (measured in seconds) and one nonverbal reaction are shown in square brackets. F's London Jamaican utterances are given in *italics*.

Example 2

F:　hey Dievid [0.8] is it t-t-true, is it t-true that
　　someone *tell* me that you go b-b-b-buildup sound
　　and *yu a go plie* at school disco
　　[0.4]

D:　yeah　　　　　　　　　　　　　　　　　　　　　　　　5
　　[0.6]

F:　well, tell [0.8] please tell me the name
　　a yu soun

D:　solomonic

F:　come on you can't use that *raas niem* that is the　　　10
　　niem of [0.9] *Dievid* Black *them* sound *jimafia* –
　　solomonic 'ow can you *tiif* someone's *niem* like
　　that man

D:　(Man) they finish
　　[0.8]　　　　　　　　　　　　　　　　　　　　　　　15

F:　look (.) *dem no finish dem mekop tuu raas*
　　different *soun wan kaal* // [0.6] *wan kaal*
　　kimafia ('n) wan kaal philharmonic

D:　*dem finish*
　　dem finish　　　　　　　　　　　　　　　　　　　20

F:　*no tel mi no bulshit about huu finish an*
　　huu no finish rait // you can't *tiifman*
　　di niem

D:　*dem finish*
　　a tiif it aaredi (.) can't do nuffink about it　　　25

F:　I think you c'd [1.0] I think you c'd
　　t-t-t-t-t-tiif C-c-coxsan *niem* (.) y-y-you
　　could go op to *Coxsan an se yu a go yuuz*
　　in niem [0.8] *an tomp im in im ed*

[2.0] [D hisses]   30
F: well it's true *man* you can't *tiif dem*
     raas niem y'know=
D: =*I'll just give you a few lyrics*

There are several interesting points to note about the speech of F. (D has relatively little to say in this extract, and I shall not comment on his speech.) First of all, not one of F's turns in the conversation is in 'pure' London English (London English throughout). Conversely, none is in 'pure' Jamaican. All of them have features distinctive of both London English and London Jamaican. However, only two utterances of F, lines 16 and 22, are *substantially* in London Jamaican. To put this another way, only these two utterances correspond closely to Jamaican Creole as spoken in Jamaica (allowing for minor differences of pronunciation.) The rest are largely tokenistic and limited to certain features of phonology, morphology and syntax that are associated with the Jamaican stereotype. In line 1, for example, F uses the Jamaican Creole *ie* pronunciation (similar to the pronunciation of *pier* in South-East England), which corresponds to received ('BBC') pronunciation [ɛɪ], in *David*, and he continues to use this pronunciation of the diphthong throughout, again in *plie* 'play' (line 3), *Dievid* (line 11) and *niem* 'name' (lines 10, 11, 12, 23, 27, 29, 32). However, he uses the London pronunciation of 'name' in line 7, although the following phrase is in Jamaican: *a yu soun* [a ju sown] rather than London English *o(f) your sound* [əjɔː sʊənd].

This type of inconsistency is thoroughly typical of conversations conducted wholly or partly in London Jamaican. F's talk throughout shows signs of adaptation towards a norm associated with a stereotype of London Jamaican, but he attains that norm only on relatively few occasions. In particular, many of his usages characterize London English only and cannot be considered part of the Jamaican system by any stretch of the imagination: for instance, the subject/auxiliary inversion in line 12 ('ow can you/Jamaican Creole *ou yu kyan*), the use of the 'dummy' *it* in line 1, again with subject/

auxiliary inversion (*is it true*/Jamaican Creole *fi truu*) and the possessive *'s* in line 13 (someone's *niem*/Jamaican Creole *smaadi niem*). Even where his utterances are at their most Jamaican, F still does not adapt as much as he could to the Jamaican Creole norm: thus *can't* in line 22 is [kʰa:n] rather than *kyaan* [ca:n], where the palatal [c] is characteristic of Jamaican Creole.

Thus it is possible to characterize the London Jamaican speech of F, and of many other black Londoners, as a set of systems that interact with each other but are also independent to the extent that, for example, an item identified as Jamaican by phonology alone may occur embedded in a sequence that is London English in its syntax, phonology and lexis (e.g. *niem* in line 11 of example 2). Some less fluent speakers, such as F, whose competence seems to be on a par with that of many other black Londoners of his age group (about 15 years old), seem to treat London Jamaican as a set of rules applied to a London English 'base' to 'convert' London English to London Jamaican. As one might expect, this 'conversion' is not always perfect: there are points where the speaker fails to apply a rule (I do not want to suggest that this happens randomly or by accident, although it sometimes may) or applies a rule inappropriately, as in example 3.

Example 3

I: aal dem pliisman breʔ di luo y'know. yu kaal dem luor
    boʔ de breʔ di luor (All them policemen break the law,
    y'know. You call them law, but they break the law.)

The misadapted item in example 3 is the word *law*. In London English, which is an 'r-less' dialect – meaning that 'r' is not pronounced after a vowel and before a consonant or at the end of the word, as in *car* or *heart* (compare the Scottish, West Country or North American pronunciations of the same word) – *poor* [pʰɔ:] and *sore* [sɔ:] rhyme with *law* [lɔ:] and *jaw* [ʤɔ:]. In contrast, in both Jamaican Creole and Jamaican Standard English word-final postvocalic *r* occurs in *poor* and *sore* but not in *law* and *jaw*. In Jamaican Creole these are *puor*, *suor*, *laa* and *jaa*. In example 3 I seems to have produced the form *luor* by applying a rule of the form [ɔ:] → [uɔɹ] to the London English form [lɔ:]. This rule, of course, gives the correct 'Jamaican' output for many words, including *poor* and *sore*, but not for *law, jaw* and other words lacking the orthographic *r*. (In an analogous misapplication of a similar rule, John F. Kennedy attempted to transform his 'r-less' Bostonian into a more standard variety of North American English by inserting postvocalic *r*; hence his references to 'Cubar' in his speeches.)

In fact I is one of the most fluent London Jamaican speakers whom I have on tape, and the fact that even he made this 'mistake' seems (in my opinion) to be powerful evidence that for many speakers London Jamaican is, as I claim, a set of adaptations that may be applied, not applied or misapplied to London English forms.

I have set out below some of the most important syntactic, morphological and phonetic features of London Jamaican. In fact, most of these are illustrated in F's speech in 2, and I have listed the lines where they occur.

Adaptation	*Example*
no past tense marker	someone tell me (line 2)
past tense marked with *did*	them did have one big argument
incompletive (i.e. continuous) aspect marked with *a*	yu a go plie (line 3)
possessive noun phrase unmarked	Dievid Black them sound (line 11)
negator *no* replaces *not*	Coxson niem (line 27)
'passive' formed without copula or -ed	dem no finish (line 16)
	wan kaal philharmonic (line 18)
I → mi	mi si im 'I saw him'
my → mi	mi niem 'my name'
your → yu	yu soun 'your sound'
he → him	im tel mi 'he told me'
his → him	im ed (line 29)
they → dem/them	dem no finish (line 16)

their → dem/them	dem (raas) niem (line 32)
dem/them used as plural marker	Dievid Black them sound (line 11)
ay [ɛɪ] → ie [ɪə]	Dievid, niem (passim)
ow [aw] → ou [ow]	soun (line 17), about (line 21)
th [θ] → t [t]	tiif (line 12), tomp (line 29)
th [ð] → d [d]	di (line 23)
u [ʌ] → o [ɔ]	tomp (line 29) mekop 'make-up' (line 16)
[ɔ:] → [a:]	kaal 'call' (line 17)
[æ] → [ɐ]	man (line 13), an (line 22)

In addition to the adaptations I have listed, there are certain lexical items and features of stress and prosody that characterize London Jamaican speech. Of the lexical items, some are taboo words like *raas* ('arse') (lines 10, 16) used mainly by males as a sort of general emphasizer, or *blodklaat*, *bomboklaat* and *raasklaat* (all meaning 'sanitary towel'), which are highly obscene, used both by males and females. Others are forms of address or attention-getters like *man* (line 13), *guy*, *bwai* ('boy'), *star* and *spa* ('friend'). All of these form part of the Jamaican stereotype and can mark a stretch of speech as 'Jamaican'. Another lexical item that not only has stereotypical value as a marker of 'Jamaican' speech but serves a further function as well is the sentence-final 'y' know'. From the frequency of this item in conversation – it sometimes ends virtually every sentence – it is clear that it plays some role that is different from that of the English tag 'you know?'. In a series of papers Local, Wells and Sebba (1983, 1984) have discussed the function of this 'y' know' in the context of London Jamaican intonation patterns. We found that in London Jamaican declarative sentences the main falling-pitch movement is usually on the final syllable. In familiar dialects of English, such as received pronunciation, pitch movement typically occurs on a focused item in the sentence, marking it as in potential contrast to another item in the same category and/or as new information. In London Jamaican these functions are achieved differently, since although the *know* of *y' know* usually has the most salient pitch movement in the sentence where it occurs – a narrow fall – participants in a conversation do not respond to *know* as if it were a focused item, e.g., by saying, 'Yes, I know.' Instead, London Jamaican reserves pitch movement for a delimitative function and uses other devices to mark items as focused. One of these is initial consonant length. The system is thus quite different from, say, received pronunciation. As regards *y' know* itself, it is strongly stereotypical of 'Jamaican' speech and is used by speakers to identify their utterances as belonging to 'Jamaican'. It is used by both males and females, (but more by males) and seems also to be associated with the Rastafarian image.

Code-Switching

It is important to understand that although London Jamaican, at least as I have described it here, is a set of norms and rules for adapting a London English base rather than a highly focused language variety (see Le Page, 1978, for a discussion of 'focusing'), nevertheless speakers themselves have a concept of 'Jamaican' or 'Patois' that is characterized by these norms and *behave* as if such a language existed. In other words, although by strictly formal linguistic criteria it may be impossible to describe the language of F in example 2 as an internally consistent system – because it shifts constantly between London English and a version of Jamaican Creole – the evidence suggests that speakers themselves behave as if there were an entity called 'Jamaican' or 'Patois' that they can use and identify, partly by means of the features described in the last section. However, for an utterance to count as, and be responded to as, London Jamaican it may be sufficient for it to have just a few of the features listed above. Some of them are much more powerful than others for the purpose of evoking the Jamaican stereotype. The sentence-final *y' know* would be near the top of the list.

There is plenty of evidence that speakers distinguish between two codes. I have on tape a number of instances of speakers correcting themselves, as in example 4:

Example 4

(a) J: you 'ave a nice day then
    C: 'course(.) [0.8] (hhhn) 'e bough? me – *im bai mi dis kiipa* [keeper?] *ring* (0.8) *guol chien*

(b) I: *dem tomp im an kil im*
    F: (fhm)
    I: an' as I said [i de?] righ?, *im iz a* – he he's a baxer innit
    F: yeah
    I: *an i kan tek lik, i kan tek gud lik*

(c) F: . . . when I talk(ed) to you last night wiv(h) Stuart you *a tel mi dat yu afi go* (0.2) d-d-d-th-that you 'ave to go get somebody one thousand watt amp

In example 4(a) the switch is from London English to London Jamaican; in (b) and (c) the switches are from London Jamaican to London English. It is remarkable that speakers should go to the effort of correcting themselves in this way when there is no reason to suppose that the original phrase would be misunderstood. There must be another motive for code-switching.

My research suggests that code-switching is used as a strategic and narrative device, as well as an additional resource for conveying affective meaning, i.e. for giving information about the attitude or state of mind of the speaker. Other studies of the motivation for code-switching have tended to concentrate on this last aspect of it, seeing it as a function of solidarity or distance between speakers, attitudes toward the subject under discussion or the social setting in which the talk takes place. While all of these play their part in determining the basic code used for interaction by young Afro-Caribbeans, there is evidence that code-switching is also affected by formal properties of conversation, such as the function of the utterance (request, agreement, disagreement, command, rebuke) or its position in the narrative. This means that although *some* code-switching is 'psychologically' motivated – for instance, in example 5, where B switches to London Jamaican to disclose what was 'in her mind', there are other criteria that determine a speaker's choice of code and relate to the mechanics of the conversation or narrative rather than the speaker's state of mind.

Example 5

B: and then I just laughed
and then 'e – 'e just pulled me for a dance
I didn't mind dancing wiv 'im
'cause *mi nuo se, mi n' av notin ina* my mind
but to dance, and then we star?ed to talk and all the rest
of it and that's it (.) *ful stap*

In general, speakers can be said to choose a code for a conversation and to stick to it. In the majority of instances this code is London English, though in certain circumstances, and especially when the participants in the talk are male, it is London Jamaican. Speakers' behaviour in conversation shows that switches of code, whether between turns (i.e. from one speaker to the next) or within a single speaker's turn are the exception rather than the rule. They do not occur haphazardly but only when there is a specific motivation for switching. Thus switches themselves have meaning in many cases. Sebba and Wootton (1984) discuss a number of different types of within-turn code-switching in London Jamaican/London English. One frequent type of switch is illustrated in example 6.

Example 6

L: *huu ena ge? aaf kuors* (Who got off-course?)
B: ie *im nou no* (.) he::: *yu slap doun i se 'pin',*
im slap doun i se 'niidl' heh
[male laughter]
B: *im slap doun im* what did you say again?
M: ha ha
B: what did you say?
M1: *krablous* (crablouse)

M2: yeh
B: *krablous*   [i:s]
L: hehehehehe
M: ha ha
B: *juk* (poke)

In this example B interrupts her own stream of London Jamaican with a question in London English. This question is very much a sideline in the sense that it is required to elicit the information B needs to complete her turn: the name that M1 gave to the domino he put down. B's switch to London English coincides with her leaving the main stream of talk (with a sentence syntactically incomplete) and her return to London Jamaican with the repetition of 'krablous' coincides with her return to complete the sentence that she left hanging. The use of London English for such self-initiated insertion sequences is common.

Code-switching also has a function in narrative. Speakers frequently switch to London Jamaican from London English, or vice versa, when repeating the speech of someone else. This apparently does not always indicate that the original speech was in the code that is used to report it; rather, the speaker seems to be using code-switching as a device to set off the reported speech from the narrative in which it is embedded.

An instance is given in example 7. Here A's London English quotation of B's earlier statement is neatly framed by London Jamaican: *a tink yu did se* before and the single word *duo* ('though') after.

Example 7
A: wha? was 'private lessons' like
    [1.8]
B: (naa) *de boy experience*   he::
A: eheh: experience *wat*
B: * *staat nou*
    [4.0]
A: *a tink yu did se* you was going to see it *duo*
    [0.6]
B: yeah, but we didn't *kach out* [2.8] you know *kaz ai woz sik an ting* you know

Another use of switching in narrative is to create a persona for a character or characters in a story. In examples I have recorded London Jamaican is used apparently to create a black persona for particular characters, while the narrator uses London English for the rest of the narrative. What is interesting is that London Jamaican is used not only to quote the speech of such characters but also *to describe the actions which characterize those individuals*; for example, in one story told by a 17-year-old boy about an incident in a shop where he worked not only the speech of the obstreperous customer is in London Jamaican (*'mi waant mi moni nou'*) but also some of the sentences describing his actions: 'a black man *kom in an im bai* a bottle of *Lukozied*', 'the man just *tomp iz fis doun'*, etc. The rest of the narrative (including certain actions of the customer) is in London English. The use of London Jamaican seems to be a narrative strategy for creating a persona for this character, though it is not applied 100 per cent consistently – perhaps because that is not necessary.

I have not been able to give anything like a complete account of why people code-switch between London English and London Jamaican. All I have done is to give a plausible account of some instances of switching and to try to show that it is systematic and related to the organization of conversation rather than linked strictly to social setting or the topic under discussion. What the foregoing suggests is that code-switching is itself a powerful linguistic resource that members of the Afro-Caribbean community have at their disposal. It not only broadens their language repertoire; it also provides additional ways of responding to other speakers, of giving praise and 'putting down', of binding together narrative and of offsetting side sequences. Naturally, members of this language community tend to use code-switching mainly among themselves, as outsiders are not likely to respond to it in appropriate ways. However, the existence of this resource is something that teachers and others who work in this community might bear in mind and that members of the community themselves might strive to preserve.

10

French Creoles in the Caribbean and Britain

MORGAN DALPHINIS

If 'Jamaican' predominates among the young, linguistic diversity among the older generation is considerable and includes French Creoles. The Caribbean's Europeans – planters, pirates, poor whites – came from Britain, Spain, Portugal, Holland and France. They imposed their 'superstrate' languages, or, as Morgan Dalphinis argues, African people took them and restructured them, making the Creoles. French Creoles have a wide distribution and, significantly, are still spoken in St Lucia, Dominica and Britain 150 years after the removal of French influence. Morgan Dalphinis indicates structural similarities between French Creoles and certain African tongues. The inference is that the Creoles are African in structure in important ways and reveal African content in their oral culture.

*Gwo Piton, Piti Piton***	*Large Piton, Small Piton*
Tjèk fwa adan lavi	Sometimes in life
Lavi ka ba nou wòch	Life hurls its stones at us,
Lavi ka ba nou fè.	Life hurls its iron at us.
Tjèk fwa adan nan vi,	Sometimes in a life,
Wòch ka pété douvan zhyé'w,	Rocks burst before your eyes,
Fè nan difé cho lavi ka kwazé'w.	Iron in life's hot fire crushes you.

* In the south-west of St Lucia (West Indies) are two volcanic hills that rise almost vertically from the sea. The larger hill is called Gwo Piton and the smaller Piti Piton. The orthography used for this poem only is the St Lucian Creole Alphabet (1981–).

Men chonzhé:	But remember:
Sé wòch asou wòch	It is stone upon stone
Ka fè gwo piton, piti piton,	Which creates the large and
Difé asou difé ka fè gwo piton	small *piton*,
sòti piti piton.	Fire upon fire which creates the
	small *piton* from the large
Mòn lavi ki nou ka monté,	*piton*.
Ban nou fè nan tjè.	
Wòch lavi nou ka pléwé,	Life's mountain which we
Ban nou difé nan tjè.	climb,
	Give us iron in the heart,
Gwo piton piti piton,	The rocks of life we cry about,
Antwé non tjè-nou,	Give us fire in the heart.
Kité nou défan sa Kawayib	
Défan ban-nou.	Large *piton*, small *piton*,
Wòch lavi, difé lavi,	Enter our hearts.
Gwo Piton, Piton nou la! Nou la!	Let us defend what Caribs
Gwo Piton, Piti Piton ...	Defended for us.
Gwo Piton, Piti Piton ...	Rocks of life, fires of life,
	Gwo Piton, Piton we are here!
	We are here!
	Gwo Piton, Piti Piton ...
	Gwo Piton, Piti Piton ...

(Morgan Dalphinis, November 1982)

Many people from the Caribbean islands of St Lucia and Dominica who are resident in Britain speak a French Creole. Their linguistic behaviour and, to a very limited extent, their culture differ from those of the majority of Caribbean peoples in Britain, who speak English Creole. In order to examine the nature of these differences and some of their implications for French Creole speakers in Britain, an overview of French Creoles is given in this chapter in terms of history, language, African influences, oral literature and the British social context.

Before attempting to describe the term 'French Creole' it is necessary to describe the term 'Creole'. The term *Crioulo* was first used in western Africa to refer to the mulatto descendants of Portuguese and Africans in the fifteenth century. With the full development of the Atlantic slave trade, the word 'Creole' (*Eng.*) (compare *Fr. Créole*)* was extended in the Caribbean to refer to slaves born in the Caribbean as opposed to those born in Africa but subsequently brought to the Caribbean as slaves. There was some overlap between the 'Portuguese' use of the term and its Caribbean usage, in that the Creole slaves born in the Caribbean were more likely to have been of mixed/mulatto descent than those newly arrived from Africa.

Like many terms to do with ethnic groupings, the term 'Creole' also referred to language from the outset, as the language spoken by the Afro-Portuguese mulattoes was also known as 'Creole': 'certain negroes and mulattoes who call themselves Portuguese . . . apart from the local language, also speak a certain jargon which has only a very slight resemblance to the Portuguese language, and which is called the creole language' (Jajolet de La Courbe [1686] in Cultru, 1913:192. The translation is my own.)

In order to draw a distinction between the earlier forms of Creole and the later, fully developed varieties, the earlier forms are called Pidgin(s), while the later varieties are called Creole(s). The main criterion for judging 'development' has so far been whether the language has become the mother tongue of a particular group. If it is not the first language of a particular group, it is called Pidgin (e.g. in the case of Nigerian Pidgin); it is called a Creole when it is the mother tongue of a group (e.g. Sierra Leone Krio, spoken as a first language by the Creoles of Freetown).

This criterion of mother tongue/first language underlines the fact that on initial contact between Africans and Europeans in Africa and the Caribbean both groups developed a

---

*The abbreviations and orthography used in this chapter are as follows: (i) abbreviations: *P.* – Patwa, *Fr.* – French, *Eng.* – English, *Neg.* – negative, *Prog.* – progressive, *pl.* – plural, *sing.* – singular, *masc.* – masculine, *Rel.* – relative, *Fut.* – future, *Complet.* – completive, *Incomplet.* – incompletive, *Hab.* – habitual, *Im.* – imminent, *Past* – past tense, *Imp.* – imperative, ' ' – free translation, " " – literal translation, → – becomes, > – derived from or more than, < – less than, ~ – in free variation with; (ii) orthography: the International African alphabet is used with the following modifications: *sh* – [ʃ] (International Phonetic Alphabet), *zh* – [ʒ] (International Phonetic Alphabet), *ng* – [ŋ] (International Phonetic Alphabet), V̄ – nasalization, V́ – stress.

trading language of restricted vocabulary in order to communicate. When the African/European mulatto population grew in size and political importance, this trading language was expanded by the vocabulary of the European language in conjunction with the grammatical structure(s) of the African language(s) involved. Where the European language concerned was French, a French Creole developed, and where English dominated, an English Creole resulted, both in western Africa and the Caribbean.

'Patwa' (*Fr. Patois*) is another term relevant to this discussion. In French the term means 'dialect'. In the French colonies the term was extended to refer, derogatorily, to the Creole language of the slaves. The majority of the slaves used the term, however, non-pejoratively, to refer to their language. English Creole speakers too now use this term.

In the French colonies, and elsewhere in the Caribbean, social structure correlated with a class/colour system in which people with more European genes and a lighter skin colour were socially more favoured, while those with more African genes and a darker skin colour were socially disadvantaged; for example, a quadroon was recognized as having four parts European parentage, while an octeroon had, or was supposed to have, eight parts European parentage. People with lighter-coloured skins were called (*Fr.*) *gens de couleur* (meaning 'people of colour') or at times *Créole*. In the following lament a St Lucian of Congolese descent mourns over such social/racial discrimination:

nu pa nã peyi nu
"we *Neg.* in country our": 'We are not in our country'

fãm Kweɔl pa vle mwɛ̃ lakai li
"woman Creole *Neg.* want me house (s)he":
'The Creole woman does not want me in her house'

In St Lucia and Martinique, both former French colonies, (*Fr.*) *Patois* (Patwa) referred to the language, while *Créole* (*P. Kweɔl, Kewɔl Kweɔl*) referred first to the lighter-skinned population but subsequently was extended to include anyone of partially African descent, in contrast to those of other ethnic groups, i.e. (*P.*) *Kuli* (East Indians) and (*P.*) *Kawayib* (Island Carib or Black Carib).

Many linguists now prefer to use the term 'Creole' to refer to the language, arguing that the term 'Patwa' is derived from the derogatory French term *Patois* and hence is offensive to the promoters of Creole nationalism. This wish to 'purify' Patwa, however, does not take into account the other derogatory French terms that have been changed to neutral, nonderogatory terms in both English and French Creoles, (e.g. *Fr. nègre* – 'negro' or 'nigger' → *P. nɛg* – 'negro' or 'person'; *Fr. bougre* – 'bugger' → *P.* 'person', while *Eng. boy* – servant → *Eng. Creole bɔi* – 'person' or 'fellow' or 'friend'). Africans in slave societies used the insults of their European slave-masters to create neutral terms to refer to themselves, probably with little or no knowledge of the original French and English usage. Their French- and English-speaking descendants, fully aware of such European usage, now wish to 'purify' their Creoles, using these European languages as a yardstick. I, however, wish to use the term 'Patwa' to refer neutrally to the French Creole of St Lucia.

French Creoles

In the discussion above French Creole was discussed as a term. In the following discussion 'creole(s)' will refer to the language(s) and 'Creole(s)' to the society and/or people.

French creoles were developed in the following Indian Ocean, Caribbean and American areas under French control (for a world list of pidgins and creoles see Hancock, 1971):

Indian Ocean	*Caribbean*	*Americas*
Mauritius	Haiti	Louisiana (North)
Réunion	Martinique	French Guyana
Seychelles	Guadeloupe	(South)
Roderigues	St Lucia	
	Dominica	
	Grenada	

Caribbean (cont.)
Carriacou and the
  Grenadines
Trinidad and
  Tobago
Désirade
Marie Galante
Les Saintes
St Barthélemy

They resulted from a mixture of the African languages of the slaves and the French language of their masters. The exact nature of this mixture is hotly debated, reflecting both the divergent linguistic philosophies of creole scholars and the varying origins of the vocabulary and grammatical structure of all creoles.

Historically, the French creoles were developed out of the necessity for communication between Africans, European and other ethnic groups (for example, Indians in Mauritius and Amerindians in the Caribbean) of different language backgrounds within the French colonies, during the period of the Atlantic slave trade. The Africans frequently, did not speak the same language, and their masters, in order to pre-empt slave revolts, often deliberately separated Africans speaking the same language and would punish any African making use of an African language.

The Africans, therefore, invented a new language to suit the limitations of their environment: using the familiar grammatical patterns of their African languages, they moulded the French vocabulary that they were forced to use to their African pronunciation patterns and concepts.

It would be difficult to give an exact date for the genesis of the French creoles, particularly as, like other creoles, they are thought to have been preceded by a pidgin (see above). It is argued by some linguists (e.g. Voorhoeve, 1971:188) that Caribbean creoles all originated from a seventeenth-century Portuguese pidgin developed on the western Africa coast. This pidgin is thought to have changed its Portuguese-derived (or relexified) vocabulary to English, French or Dutch vocabulary, depending upon whether the Portuguese pidgin-speaking Africans were brought to an English, a French or a Dutch colony.

Although this would suggest a greater emphasis upon a single European language (i.e. Portuguese) in the development of all the Caribbean creoles, this Portuguese pidgin itself was a mainly African creation, modelled on the African grammatical structures of the African languages of the Afro-Portuguese mulattos in western Africa (see Allsopp, 1976, and Dalphinis, 1981:54–85).

Historical references to the French creoles, however, may generally point to the presence of a late sixteenth-century French pidgin, corresponding to the beginnings of the Atlantic slave trade and the French Caribbean colonies, and of a late eighteenth-century French creole, corresponding to the expansion of the Atlantic slave trade and the fuller development of the French Caribbean colonies.

Inhabitants still speak French creoles in the areas where they were originally developed (see above) with the exception of Trinidad, Grenada and the Grenadines and Louisiana, where they are dying languages spoken by the older members of these communities. An important aspect of the gradual disappearance of these three creoles is that they lost close contact with their formative European language, French, when English speakers took over the political control of these creole territories. In St Lucia and Dominica, however, the majority of the inhabitants still speak creole despite similar separation from French.

In areas where French is still spoken (i.e. Haiti, Guadeloupe, Martinique, Désirade, Marie Galante, Les Saintes, St Barthélemy, French Guyana, Mauritius, Réunion, Seychelles and Roderigues) French creoles retain more of their original French vocabulary than French creoles no longer in synchronic (contemporary) contact with French (e.g. in Martinique *liv la*, Fr. *le livre* – 'the book', while in St Lucia and Dominica *liv la~buk la* – 'the book').

In the case of Trinidad and Grenada this process of change

in vocabulary from French- to English-derived (i.e. relexification) is historically so advanced that it has aided the gradual disappearance of French creole in both islands.

Variations among the French creoles also exist at the level of grammar. These grammatical variations are due mainly to ethnic differences in the early pidgin speakers in the different former French colonies. Just as the first language used by a child contributes more determinedly to the child's linguistic make-up than do subsequent languages, so also did the first populations using French pidgin/creole have a more determining effect upon the language habits of subsequent slave and other migrant groups in the former French colonies.

For example, Réunion creole grammar is different from Mauritian creole grammar. Réunion creole grammar is more similar to French grammar than Mauritian creole, which is closer to Haitian than the former. As the majority of the early Réunion population were French, in contrast to the early African population of Mauritius and Haiti, it is likely that such grammatical differences may signal differences in ethnicity (P. Baker, pers. comm., 1980).

St Lucian French creole is distinct from Haitian creole at different points of grammatical structure, e.g.:

St Lucian: *mwẽ   ka   vini*
             "I   Prog. come":   'I am coming'

Haitian: *m   ap   vini*
             "I   Prog. come":   'I am coming'

As the early St Lucian population comprised mainly Mandinka speakers from Senegambia and the early Haitian population comprised Ewe/Fon speakers from the kingdom of Dahomey (Dalphinis, 1981:pt III, ch. 1; Comhaire-Sylvain, 1936), and as St Lucian *ka* is possibly derived from Mandinka *ka* – Prog. (Dalphinis, 1981:483), it is likely that this difference in grammar is related to the ethnic differences in the early population of each island.

St Lucian Patwa: A French Creole in Britain

In order to give brief exemplification of a French creole that has been brought to Britain, the St Lucian variety (I am a native speaker) is outlined below in terms of language, influences and social background.

Language

Some of the main features of this language are outlined below (though see Carrington, 1967, and Dalphinis, 1981, for a fuller description of St Lucian Patwa).

Consonants In the table below the vertical column on the left refers to the type of sound made, and the horizontal column headings refer to the place in the mouth where the sound is produced: labial – the lips; dental – the teeth; alveolar – the ridge behind the teeth; palatal – the hard palate; velar – the soft palate; glottal – the vocal cords.

	Bilabial	Labio dental	Dental/ alveolar	Alveolo- palatal	Velar	Glottal
Plosive	p b		t d	c j	k g	
Nasal	m		n		ng	
Lateral (non-fricative)			l			
Rolled					r	
Fricative		f v	s z	sh zh		
Semi-vowels	w			y		h

Vowels These are produced at the front or the back of the mouth, as follows:

      Front   *i e ɛ a*
      Back   u o ɔ

Of these vowels the following have nasal varieties:

Front $\tilde{\varepsilon}$ $\tilde{a}$
Back $\tilde{ɔ}$

For example:
fɛ – 'to make' (as in *Eng.* bed)
fɛ̃ – 'to be hungry' (as in *Eng* sense)
ba – 'to give' (as in *Eng.* *a*t)
bã – 'bench' (as in *Eng.* *a*nxious)
tɔ – 'fault' (as in *Eng.* f*aw*n)
tɔ̃ – 'tuna fish' (as in *Eng.* continue)

These consonants and vowels may be combined to form nouns, pronouns, adjectives and verbs.

Nouns The definite article (equivalent to *Eng.* 'the') appears after the noun, for example:

liv   la
"book the": 'the book'

kai   la
"house the": 'the house'

kle   a
"key the": 'the key'

As in any creole and African language, the Patwa noun has a single form, even in the plural, which is formed by placing *se* in front of the noun and its following definite article, for example:

se liv la
"*pl.* book the": 'the books'

se kai la
"*pl.* house the": 'the houses'

se kle a
"*pl.* key the": 'the keys'

Pronouns The Patwa subject pronouns are as follows:

	1	2	3
Singular	*mwɛ̃* or *ng-*	*u*	*i* or *li*
Plural	*nu*	*zɔt*	*jo*

For example:

> *mwɛ̃ vini*
> "I   come": 'I come'
>
> *nga   vini*
> "I Prog. come": 'I am coming'
>
> *i   vini*
> "s/he come": 's/he comes'
>
> *li   vini*
> "s/he come": 's/he comes'

Adjectives These may precede or follow the noun. For example:

> *ã bɛl   tifi*
> "a beautiful girl": 'a beautiful girl'
>
> *tifi a bɛl*
> "girl the beautiful": 'the girl is beautiful'

Verbs Like nouns, verbs have one form only except for a small class of verbs indicating intensity, which have the prefix *dé-*. For example:

mɔde – 'to bite'	*démɔde* – 'to bite to pieces'
viwe – 'to return'	*déviwe* – 'to go to and fro'

Nouns, pronouns, adjectives and verbs may be combined with a number of verbal markers to form the basic type of Patwa clause, as follows (the bracketed items are optional):

subject:		(verbal markers)			verb	(object:
noun or						noun or
pronoun	(relative)	(negative)	(tense)	(aspect)		pronoun)

Verbal markers in Patwa precede the verb.

The relative *ki* may follow any item in subject position to form a relative clause:

> *liv   la   ki   bwile*
> "book the *Rel.* burn": 'the book that burns'

Except in the case of the first person singular, *mwɛ̃*, the negative is formed by placing *pa* before the verb:

> *i   pa   bɛl*
> "s/he *Neg.* beautiful": 's/he is not beautiful/handsome'

The first person singular has its own negative forms, for example:

> *ma vini*
> "I *Neg.* come": 'I did not come'

(See Dalphinis, 1981:439–41, for a full description of Patwa first singular negative forms.)

The past (*te*) and non-imminent future (*kai*) tense markers are used thus:

> *i   te   ale*
> "s/he *Past* go": 's/he went'
> *i   kai ale*
> "s/he *Fut.* go": 's/he will go'

Examples of the use of Patwa aspect markers – *zha* or *za* (*Complet.*), *pɔkɔ* (*Incomplet.*), ø (*Neutral* – no marker), *ka* (*Prog.*), *ka* (*Hab.*) and *ka* (*Fut. Im.*) – are the following:

i   zha/za   vini
"s/he *Complet.* come": 's/he has come'

i   pɔkɔ   vini
"s/he *Incomplet.* come": 's/he has not yet come'

i   ø   vini
"s/he *Neutral* come": 's/he comes/came'

i   ka   vini
"s/he *Prog.* come": 's/he is coming'

yo   ka   dɔmi isi
"they *Hab.* sleep here": 'they (habitually) sleep here'

i   ka   vini
"s/he *Fut. Im.* come": 's/he is coming right now'

African Influences

African influences in French creoles in general and in St Lucian Patwa in particular can be considered from the viewpoints of vocabulary, grammar and oral literature.

Vocabulary   As the use of African languages was outlawed in past French Creole societies, few words directly reflecting their African origins survived. Yet it is a measure of African cultural resistance that a number of African words, indicative of the different origins of the African slaves in these French Creole communities, did survive and persist to this day in French Creole speech in St Lucia and elsewhere:

St Lucian Patwa	African languages
bi – 'piece'	Twi/Fante *bi* – 'piece'
twɛ̃ – 'quarrel'	TwiFante *twɛ̃* – 'to quarrel'
tim tim – opening formula for prose narratives	Mandinka and Diola *taling taling* – 'ditto'
okayi – 'woman'	Umbundu *ukayi* – 'woman'
okadimba – 'goat', 'sheep'	Umbundu *okandimba* – 'goat', 'sheep'

Some African words have had their meanings extended – for example, St Lucian Patwa *jabal* ('loose woman', 'paramour'), cf. Wolof *jabar* ('wife'); Martinique French creole *angulu* ('greedy person'), cf. Hausa *ungulu* ('vulture') – and some have converged or merged their identity with French words of similar form and/or meaning. For example:

St Lucian Patwa	French	African languages
ba – 'to give'	*baillir* – 'to give'	Hausa *ba* – 'to give'
bug – 'person'	*bougre* – 'heretic'	
ɛk – 'with'	*avec* – 'with'	Mandinka *baga* – 'person'
		Wolof *ak* – 'and'

Other words in St Lucian Patwa and other French creole languages reflect the meaning of African words, although their forms are similar to those of French words. For example:

St Lucian Patwa	French	African languages
go zhye	gros yeux	Igbo *anya uku*
"big eye"	'big eyes'	"eye big"
'greedy'		'greedy'
ashte lamẽ	*acheter du main*	Hausa *sayo . . . hannu*
"buy hand"	'buy from the	"buy . . . hand"
'to buy from'	hand'	'to buy from'
kɔ̃ di	*comme si*	Mandinka *a ko*
"like say"	'as if'	"it say"
'as if'		'as if'

Grammar Like most other French creoles, St Lucian Patwa owes its genesis, at least in part, to the creative needs of Africans deprived of the public use of their languages. Constrained by the social circumstances of slavery, the Africans made use of the vocabulary of the French language of their masters coupled with the grammars of their various African languages. Where the grammars of the African languages were convergent their grammatical structures became more acceptable to a higher proportion of the African population.

In French creoles the definite article follows the noun, as we have seen:

> liv   la   (cf. *Fr. le livre*)
> "book the":'the book'
>
> tab   la   (cf. *Fr. la table*)
> "table the": 'the table'

Although the vocabulary is evidently French, the position of the definite article *la* reflects the grammatical structure of the two numerically most important groups in the early African population of French Creole societies, the Mandinka and the Wolof. In both the Mandinka and the Wolof language the definite article also follows the noun. For example:

> Mandinka   *jɔng*   *ɔ*
> "slave the": 'the slave'
>
> Wolof   *gɔr*   *gi*
> "man the": 'the man'

Mandinka grammatical structure is also reflected in St Lucian Patwa and the French creoles of Martinique and Guadeloupe. For example:

St Lucian Patwa   *mwɛ̃ ka mãzhe*
"I *Prog.* eat": 'I am eating'

Mandinka   *ng ka moi*
"I *Prog.* understand": 'I understand'

Martinique *Fr.* Creole *i ke vini*
"s/he *Prog.* come": 's/he is coming'

Mandinka (Gambian *ng ke moi*
dialect)
"I *Prog.* understand": 'I understand'

As I have noted, the African languages that were first imported into the French colonies had a more determining effect than subsequent ones. As a consequence, African languages imported later – for example, Umbundu and Twi/Fante – contributed more to the vocabulary than to the structure of St Lucian Patwa and other French creoles, which had already been established by the Wolof and the Mandinka. Nevertheless, similar grammatical structures in these later languages reinforced structures that were already in place in the French creoles. For example, Twi/Fante *re* (*Prog.*), as in the following example:

> mɛ re   kɔ
> "I *Prog.* go": 'I am going'

could only have structurally reinforced the Mandinka progressive *ka* in St Lucian Patwa.

Oral literature   Oral literature in most Creole societies is often an index of their African past, in which literature was also disseminated orally. As African experts in oral literature and other fields were not encouraged in the slave systems of French Creole societies, oral literature requiring such experts (for example, the Sunjata epic of the Mandinka griots) did not survive in creole oral literature of any Caribbean society.

The oral literature of the majority in many African societies, however, was transmitted into French creole oral literature, particularly prose narratives, proverbs, riddles and songs. Note, for example, the similarities between the following proverb in St Lucian Patwa and the African language:

Hausa *In ka*   *ga gemun d'an uwanka*
    "If you (masc. sing.) see beard of son mother you

      ya kama wuta, ka   shafa wa naka ruwa.
      it catch fire,   you throw on yours water

St Lucian *Si u*   *wɛ bab   kamawad-u pwi*
Patwa   "If you (masc. sing.) see beard friend you   catch

> *dife, voye glo   asu sa-u*
> fire throw water on that you."

St Lucian 'Take precautions against misfortunes that people
whom you know have suffered.'

The French creole tale about *kɔ̃pɛ lapɛ̃* (Brer Rabbit), who
hides in a cow's intestines with *kɔ̃pɛ tig* (Brer Tiger), is similar
to a Wolof/Mandinka tale about Brer Rabbit (cf. Wolof
leuk), who hides with a hyena in the intestines of an elephant.
Similarly, there is a Brer Rabbit cycle of tales both in the
French creoles and in a number of other western African
languages, including Hausa and Kikongo (see Monteil,
1905:45–9; Dorson, 1967:82–3, in which a similar Afro-
American tale is described; Dalphinis, 1981:150–1).

French creole songs resemble their African language orig-
inals in their 'call-and-refrain' structure, in which a lead
singer sings the main song and the refrain is sung by a chorus,
as in this French creole example:

CHORUS: *U   wɛ u   wɛ bagai sa   la*
"You (*sing.*) see you (*sing.*) see thing that this

'See, see this thing!

(Repeat three times)

LEAD: *bagai sa   la   Ivawis fɛ a*
thing that this Ivawis do the

CHORUS: (Sings once as above)

LEAD: *Saupose ti   Ivawis maye*
Suppose little Ivawis marry"

Even if little Ivawis marries'

CHORUS: (Sings once as above) ...

French creole oral literature has also functioned as an
important archive for words from African languages; the

African words in Patwa (see above), for example, are mainly from Patwa oral literature (see Dalphinis, 1981:pt III, ch. 6).

Society

Like other Caribbean societies, St Lucian society resulted from a slave-based plantation system within which Europeans (first the French and subsequently the English) formed the ruling elite; mulattoes and 'free blacks' (*gens de couleur*) formed the middle-ranking group and the Africans the majority low-prestige group.

This pyramidal social model has had a determining effect on all facets of the society, both in the past and in the present (see Fanon, 1967; Williams, E., 1964; James, 1963; Dalphinis, 1981:pt III, ch. 1). As far as language is concerned, this social model resulted in a creole language of low prestige being spoken by the people of African descent (i.e. *Kweɔl ~Keɔl* in St Lucian Patwa) in contact with French, spoken by the French rulers of St Lucia until about 1834, and then in contact with English, spoken from this period by the British, who finally took over from the French in St Lucia.

With the increasing loss of contact between the St Lucian ruling groups and their respective metropoles (France and then Britain), the Patwa language became the language that was most widely spoken, or at least the most widely understood, by the members of the society, including the rulers.

The pyramidal social structure, nevertheless, left its mark: the ruling groups did not use Patwa as a vehicle of communication between themselves (French and, later on, English were preferred). Patwa was, however, used by members of the ruling group to their social inferiors. As a consequence, even in relatively recent times people of low social status spoke Patwa freely among themselves but resented it if a person of higher social status addressed them in Patwa.

Creole nationalism of the present times has modified this negative attitude towards Patwa, which is now being increasingly used over the radio in St Lucia. The increase in the number of Patwa/English bilinguals has also had an effect, partly as a result of an English-language-based education system. As Patwa monolingualism has decreased, so the development of a Patwa that makes use of English loans (a relexified Patwa) has accelerated. The following sentences, for example, all have the same meaning:

Patwa	*gas*	*a*	*ka*	*mãzhe*	*pimã*
	"boy	the	*Prog.*	eat	pepper"
Relexified Patwa	*bɔi*	*la*	*ka*	*mãzhe*	*pimã*
	bɔi	*la*	*ka*	*it*	*pimã*
	bɔi	*la*	*ka*	*it*	*pɛpə*
	bɔi	*la*	*dɔz*	*it*	*pɛpə*
	"boy	the	*Prog.*	eat	pepper"

'The boy is eating pepper.'

This change in vocabulary underlines the social changes in a St Lucian society that responded once to the political dominance of France and then to British political aims. It may now, with its recent independence, reflect both St Lucian- and Patwa-orientated aspirations, coupled with those of the largely English and English-creole-speaking Caribbean Economic Community, of which St Lucia is a member. The ideology and economic power of the neighbouring USA, coupled with its international language, English, may increase the number of English loans in Patwa and the other French creoles. This development will, however, be affected by the degree of patriotism of French creole speakers and the value they place upon their own language.

French Creoles in Britain and the Development of a British Black Society

French creole speakers came to Britain with other West Indian immigrant workers in the early 1950s. They settled mainly in the London areas of Hackney and Paddington, and in Bradford (where French creole speakers are mainly Dominicans).

As they are a minority within the larger English creole-speaking groups of which Jamaicans are the majority, their language has remained an in-group language only, even more than English creole. This is not unrelated to the fact that, as English is the most widely spoken international language, creoles with an English-based lexicon have generally become more diffused than the French creoles. This diffusion of English creoles has been aided by the spread of reggae songs in English creole among non-speakers of English creole. As a consequence, in Britain French creoles are used between French creole speakers only, often in private but also publicly, in order not to be understood by English, French and English creole speakers.

Partly because of the vocabulary shared by Jamaican creole, the other English creoles of the Caribbean and the English language, the formation of a British black English has resulted, in which Caribbean creole English and the anglicized variants are usable (Sutcliffe, 1982). No such variation has resulted in the case of French creole in Britain. Instead there exist degrees of competence in French creole ranging from full competence, to partial competence, passive competence and, finally, non-competence. These degrees of competence may be related to age group and immigrant status in the French Creole community:

Competence	Age group	Immigrant status
Full	42 >	Immigrant
Partial	22 >	Immigrant
Passive	< 21	Non-immigrant (i.e. British-born)
None	Second-generation (all age groups)	Non-immigrant

Although anomalies may exist – e.g. the 21-year-old French Creole who speaks fluent French creole and has only recently arrived in Britain – dwindling competence in the language indicates the potential death of French creole in Britain. Just as Africans brought to the Caribbean lost their languages in favour of a community-wide creole language, so French creole speakers in Britain may gradually lose their language in favour of the West Indian, community-wide English creole and, possibly, British black English.

The island orientation of West Indian immigrants in Britain, who traditionally saw themselves as separate island groups (St Lucians, Jamaicans, Grenadians, etc.), is fast changing, in the face of the racial categories available in British society (i.e. 'black'/'white'), towards a 'black' orientation. Patterns of language use are thus following political trends. Despite the political trends, however, French creole remains the vehicle of the African/Caribbean cultural values of a distinct group among the Caribbean community in Britain. Although Caribbean culture is common to both English and French creole speakers, there are a few areas of cultural difference that affect language use.

French Creoles shared in the French Revolution, which in the Caribbean resulted in the first black independent state in the 'New World' (Haiti) and revolts culminated in the overthrow of the planter/mulatto class and the guillotine for many former slave masters (for example, in Martinique and St Lucia in 1791).

This cultural background has permeated the independent outlook of French creole speakers on language. It is therefore no accident that among this minority within the Caribbean minority in Britain the French Creoles who strive for language skills often attain an independent mastery of English and other languages. Their use of English is often of an English independent of English creole and British black English influences.

Cultural background is not the only factor in such language usage. French creole in Britain has lost contact with its formative European language, and consequently a truly bilingual background permeates the use/non-use of French creole, which is viewed as an entity independent of English by both users and non-users. By contrast, French creoles used in French-speaking areas (e.g. France, Mauritius, the Seychelles, Réunion and Guadeloupe) are used with some degree of approximation to French in the same way as English creoles are used in approximation to English in Britain. This approximation results in a non-independent use of the creoles, and their users may find it difficult to determine at which end of the continuum that extends between creole English (English-based creole) and British English they are operating.

It is perhaps the distinctiveness of the French creoles in a standard/creole English environment that results in separate domains for the use/non-use of French creole, creole English and English, as outlined below:

Language	Domain
English	Formal communication with English and English creole speakers
English creole	English creole speakers in an informal setting
British black English	Second-generation Caribbean peoples in Britain
French creole	Formal and informal communication with French creole speakers

The use/non-use of French creole in a French or former-French territory is affected by the degree of familiarity between the speakers; some speakers may, for example, be offended if greeted in French creole by someone they do not know because they view French creole as a language of informal usage and of lower prestige than English. In Britain, however, familiarity/non-familiarity and solidarity/non-solidarity are related to colour. As a consequence, a black person, especially one speaking French creole, is immediately someone with whom familiarity and solidarity are exchanged.

The present status of French creole as a minority language in Britain is reflected by its restricted usage as well as its structure. As it is not spoken in the proximity of French in Britain, its structure has to some extent been 'frozen' in the minds of the immigrants who learned it in the Caribbean or elsewhere outside Britain. French creole speakers whose creole already had many or few English loan words, for example, continue to speak these varieties of French creole in Britain, while differences between urban and rural French creole have also remained 'frozen' in the language structure of the French Creole immigrants.* The low social status of most Caribbean immigrants in Britain also contributes to the continued perception of the French creoles as 'low-status' languages.

In the Caribbean there is a wish among many creole speakers to 'modernize' themselves and their language use, partly by not speaking their languages or by adding to them as much French or English vocabulary as possible. In Britain, however, the limitations of this colonial fantasy have become clear to a number of creole speakers, who do their best to speak their languages as often as possible. Yet this general psychology of 'decreolization' and perhaps 'denegrification' has also been imported into Britain by the older generation of creole speakers who, although speaking the language among themselves, do not speak it to members of the younger generation who, they believe, will succeed in becoming 'modernized' at a faster rate if they do not speak any creole language. Africans in the Caribbean were forced to give up their African languages under the threat and practice of torture, murder and separation from their families. Ironically, Creole communities world-wide, accused of 'illiteracy', 'backwardness' and 'retardation', have volunteered to give up their languages without the resistance or the creative alternatives fought for by their African and other ancestors.

French creole oral literature, although still available in Britain, has an even more restricted use here than it had in urban areas in the Caribbean. Urban life in Britain and elsewhere militates against family meetings, wakes, boat racing and dancing of the type that formed the social context for

---

*These observations are based on preliminary research by me into the French creole of St Lucians and Dominicans in Hackney, London, October 1978.

the dissemination of French creole oral literature. It remains, however, a creative part of everyday French creole speech, even in urban areas, as it is assumed by creole speakers to be part of each other's common knowledge. For example, exclamations of encouragement from French creole oral literature are a welcome part of French creole speech in urban areas like London as well as in mainly rural St Lucia:

Chebe i fɔ   jan   Vye   Fɔ !
"Hold it hard people Vieux- Fort"
'Hold on hard to the gift of life, people of Vieux-Fort!'

Bibliography

Agard, J. (1984), *see News for Babylon*

Allsopp, R. (1976), 'The Case for Afrogenesis', paper presented to the Conference of the Society for Caribbean Linguistics, University of Guyana

Asika, N. (1984), *see News for Babylon*

Bailey, B. (1966), *Jamaican Creole Syntax: A Transformational Approach* (Cambridge: Cambridge University Press)

Bannister, D., and Fransella, F. (1971), *Inquiring Man* (Harmondsworth: Penguin Books)

Beckwith, M. W. (1929), *Black Roadways: A Study of Jamaican Folk Life* (Chapel Hill, North Carolina; University of North Carolina Press)

Bender, I., and Hastorf, A. (1950), 'The Perception of Persons: Forecasting Another Person's Responses on Three Personality Scales', *Journal of Abnormal and Social Psychology*, 45

Bennett, L. (1957), *Dialect Verse* (Kingston, Jamaica: Pioneer)

Bennett, L. (1966), *Anancy Stories* (Kingston, Jamaica: Sangsters)

Bernstein, B. (1971), *Class, Codes and Control*, vols 1 and 2 (London: Routledge & Kegan Paul)

Berry, J. (1979), *Fractured Circles* (London: New Beacon Books)

Berry, J. (1984), *see News for Babylon*

Berry, J. (1985), *Chain of Days* (Oxford: Oxford University Press)

Black, C. (1958), *History of Jamaica* (London: Collins)

Blacksheep, J. (1984), *see News for Babylon*. 'Discrimination' first appeared in *Black Eye Perceptions*, 1981 (London: Black Ink)

Bloom, V. (1984), *see News for Babylon*

Bones, J. (1979), 'Afro-Lingua: the Basis of a Rasta Language', *The Voice of Rasta*, 13

Braithwaite, E. R. (1959), *To Sir With Love* (London: The Bodley Head)

Brathwaite, E. (1973), *The Arrivants* (Oxford: Oxford University Press)

Brathwaite, E. (1982), *Sun Poem* (Oxford: Oxford University Press)

Breinburg, P. (1984a), 'Linguistic Shift – Urban Creoles and the Black Child in European Inner-City Schools', *York Papers in Linguistics*, 2

Breinburg, P. (1984b), 'Cultural Racism and Books', *Dragon's Teeth*, 19

Breinburg, P. (1984c), 'Exploring Failure in Language and Education: a Comparative Study', unpublished Ph.D. submitted to Keele University

Breman, P., and Seymour, A. (1973), *You Better Believe It* (Harmondsworth: Penguin Books)

Brunner, J. (1958), 'Social Psychology and Perception', in E. Maccoby et al. (eds), *Readings in Social Psychology* (London: Methuen)

Brunswik, E. (1956), *Perception and the Representative Design of Psychological Experiments* (Berkeley, California: University of California Press)

Burford, B. (1984), *A Dangerous Knowing* (London: Sheba)

Burns, A. (1954), *History of the British West Indies* (London: Allen & Unwin)

Campbell, H. (1979), 'Rastafarian Culture, from Garvey to Rodney', paper presented to the Society for Caribbean Studies Conference, University of Sussex

Cantril, M. (1968), 'The Nature of Social Perception', in H. Toch and H. Smith (eds), *Social Perception* (New York: Van Nostrand)

Carrington, L. D. (1967), 'St Lucian Creole: A Descriptive Analysis of its Phonology and Morphosyntax', Ph.D. thesis, University of the West Indies

Carter, H., and Sutcliffe, D. (1982), 'Pitch Patterns of a Jamaican Speaker', parts I and II, paper given to the Paramaribo conference of the Society for Caribbean Linguistics, Paramaribo.

Cashmore, E. (1977), 'The Rastaman Cometh', *New Society*, 25 August

Cassidy, F. G., and Le Page, R. B. (1980), *Dictionary of Jamaican English*, 2nd edn (Cambridge: Cambridge University Press)

Comhaire-Sylvain, S. (1936), *Le Créole haitien: morphologie et syntaxe* (Wetteren: De Meester; Port-au-Prince, Haiti)

Commission for Racial Equality (1978), *Five Views of Multi-Racial Britain* (London: CRE/BBC)

Cook, M. (1979), *Perceiving Others: The Psychology of Interpersonal Perception* (London: Methuen)

Dalphinis, M. (1981), 'African Language Influences in Creole Lexically Based on Portuguese, English and French, with Special Reference to Casamance Kriul, Gambian Krio and St Lucian Patois', unpublished Ph.D. thesis, School of Oriental and African Studies, University of London

Dhondy, F. (1982), *The Black Explosion in British Schools* (London: Race Today Collective)

Dodgson, E., and Smith, M. (1982), 'Motherland', *Ambit*, 91

Dorson, R. (ed.) (1967), *American Negro Folktales* (New York: Fawcett)

Durrant, C. (1984), *see News for Babylon*

Edwards, V. K. (1979), 'The Role of Dialect in the School', *Education Journal* (Commission for Racial Equality), 11, 1

Edwards, V. K., and Sutcliffe, D. (1985), *Language Selection in a British Black Community*, final report to the Economic and Social Science Council, London

Fanon, F. (1967), *Black Skin, White Masks* (New York: Grove Press)

Fraser, R., and Berry, J. (1981), *This Island Place* (London: Harrap)

Garcia Marquez, G. (1982), *El Olor de la Guyaba* (Barcelona: Brugera)

Giles, H., and St Clair, R. (1979), *Language and Social Psychology*, vol. 1 (Oxford: Blackwell)

Gumperz, J. (1982), *Discourse Strategies* (Cambridge: Cambridge University Press)

Hall, S. (1978), 'Racism and Reaction', in Commission for Racial Equality (1978)

Hancock, I. F. (1971), 'A Survey of the Pidgins and Creoles of the World', in D. Hymes (ed.), *Pidginization and Creolization of Languages* (Cambridge: Cambridge University Press)

Hemenway, R. (1982), 'Author, Teller and Hero', introduction to *Uncle Remus, His Songs and His Sayings* (Harmondsworth: Penguin Books)

Hewitt, R. (1982), 'White Adolescent Creole Users and the Politics of Friendship', *Journal of Multilingual and Multicultural Development*, 3, 3

Hylton, P. (1975), 'The Politics of Caribbean Music', in *The Black Scholar*, September

Jajolet de la Courbe, M. (1913), *Premier voyage du Sieur de la Courbe à la coste d'Afrique en 1685* (Paris: Cultru)

James, C. (1963), *The Black Jacobins* (New York: Vintage)

James, C. (1969), *Beyond a Boundary* (London: Hutchinson)

Johnson, A. (1984), *see News for Babylon*

Johnson, D. (1984), *Deadly Ending Season* (London: Akira)

Johnson, L. K. (1975), *Dread Beat and Blood* (London: Bogle L'Ouverture)

Johnson, L. K. (1976), 'Jamaican Rebel Music', *Race and Class*, 17, 4

Johnson, L. K. (1980), *Inglan is a Bitch* (London: Race Today)

Kay, J. (1984), *A Dangerous Knowing* (London: Sheba)

Keens-Douglas, P. (1979), *When Moon Shine* (Port-of-Spain: Keensdee)

Kelly, G. (1955), *The Psychology of Personal Construct*, vol. 2 (New York: W. W. Norton)

King, M. L. (1968), *Chaos or Community?* (New York: Harper & Row)

Kizerman, R. (1984), *see News for Babylon*

Kochman, T. (1981), 'Classroom Modalities', in Neil Mercer (ed.), *Language in School and Community* (London: Edward Arnold)

Labov, W. (1972), 'Language in the Inner City', in *Studies of Black English Vernacular* (Oxford: Blackwell)

Lamming, G. (1953), *In the Castle of My Skin* (London: Michael Joseph)

Lamming, G. (1954), *The Emigrants* (London: Michael Joseph)

Lamming, G. (1960), *Pleasures of Exile* (London: Macmillan)

Le Page, R. B. (1978), *Projection, Focusing, Diffusion, or Steps Towards a Sociolinguistic Theory of Language*, Occasional Paper No. 9, Society for Caribbean Linguistics, University of the West Indies, St Augustine

Likert, R. (1967), 'The Method of Constructing an Attitude Scale', in M. Fishbein (ed.), *Attitude Theory and Measurement* (New York: Wiley)

Local, J. K., et al. (1983), 'Turn Delimitation in London Jamaican', typescript

Local, J. K., et al. (1984), 'Phonetic Aspects of Turn Delimitation in London Jamaican', *York Papers in Linguistics*, 11, papers from the York Creole Conference, University of York, 1983

Lorimer, D. A. (1978), *Colour, Class and the Victorians* (Leicester: Leicester University Press)

Markham, E. A. (1984), *see News for Babylon*

Martin, D. (1982), *City Lines* (London: ILEA)

Miles, R. (1978), 'Between Two Cultures? The Case of Rastafarianism', *Working Paper on Ethnic Relations*, 10, Social Science Research Council, Bristol

Monteil, C. (1905), *Contes Soudanais* (Paris)

Morris, M. (1977), *Sunday Times*, 10 October

Morris, S. (1973), *Black Studies*, course booklet (London: COBS)

Naipaul, V. S. (1959), *Miguel Street* (Harmondsworth: Penguin Books)

Nelson, E. (1984), *see News for Babylon*

Nettleford, R., et al. (1960), *The Rastafarian Movement in Kingston, Jamaica* (Kingston, Jamaica: Institute of Social and Economic Studies, University of the West Indies)

News for Babylon (1984), a collection of writings (London: Chatto & Windus)

Nichols, G. (1984), *see News for Babylon*

Onuora, O. (Orlando Wong) (1977), *Echo* (Kingston, Jamaica: Sangsters)

Payne, F. (1978), 'We Want to Make Proper Patties', *TLK*, 11. Available from 79 Ronald Road, London N5

Peach, R. (1968), *West Indian Migration to Britain. A Social Geography* (London: Oxford University Press/Institute of Race Relations)

Peters, D. (1984), *see News for Babylon*

Phizacklea, A. (1975), 'A Sense of Political Efficacy: a Comparison of Black and White Adolescents', in Ivor Crewe (ed.), *British Political Sociology Yearbook: The Politics of Race* (London: Croom Helm)

Pollard, V. (1976), 'The Dust – a Tribute to the Folk', *Journal of Creole Studies*, 1, 2

Press Gang (1978), *Movement of Jah People* (Birmingham: Press Gang)

Ramchand, K., et al. (1976), *West Indian Narrative* (Sudbury: Thomas Nelson)

Rand, J. (1984), *see News for Babylon*

RAPP (1984), *see News for Babylon*

Reid, V. (1973), *New Day* (London: Heinemann)

Reisman, K. (1974), 'Contrapuntal Conversations in an Antiguan Village', in R. Bauman and J. Sherzer (eds), *Exploration in the Ethnography of Speaking* (Cambridge: Cambridge University Press)

Ryan, E., and Giles, H. (1982), *Attitudes Towards Language Variations: Social and Applied Contexts* (London: Edward Arnold)

Salkey, A., et al. (1960), *West Indian Stories* (London: Faber & Faber)

Scobie, E. (1972), *Black Britannia: A History of Blacks in Britain* (Chicago: Johnson)

Sealy, R. (1978), 'Through Autumn to Summer' (London: Vauxhall Manor School)

Sebba, M. (1984a), 'Serial Verb or Syntactic Calque: the Great Circuit of *se*', paper presented to the Society for Caribbean Linguistics, Mona, Jamaica

Sebba, M., and Wootton, A. J. (1984b), 'Conversational Code Switching in London Jamaican', paper presented at the Fifth Sociolinguistics Symposium, Liverpool

Selvon, S. (1956), *Lonely Londoners* (London: MacGibbon)

Shyllon, F. O. (1974), *Black Slaves in Britain* (Oxford: Oxford University Press/Institute of Race Relations)

Simpson, G. E., and Yinger, J. M. (1965), *Racial and Cultural Minorities*, 3rd edn (New York: Harper & Row)

Sivanandan, A. (1976), 'Race, Class and the State: the Black Experience in Britain', *Race and Class*, 1

Skyers, B. (1982), *City Lines* (London: ILEA)

Smitherman, G. (1981), *Talkin' and Testifyin': The Language of Black America* (New York: Houghton Mifflin)

Snead, J. (1984), 'Repetition as a Figure of Black Culture', in H. Gates (ed.), *Black Literature and Literature Theory* (New York: Methuen)

Stead, C., and d'Aguiar, F. (1982), *It's Now* (Lumb Bank: Course 20)

Stoops, Y. (forthcoming), *Comparative Study of Afrikaans and Dutch*

Sutcliffe, D. (1978), 'The Language of First and Second Generation West Indian Children in Bedfordshire', Ph.D. thesis, University of Leicester. Available also from the British Lending Library, Leamington Spa

Sutcliffe, D. (1982), *British Black English* (Oxford: Blackwell)

Tafari, L. (1984), *see News for Babylon*

Taguiri, R. (1969), 'Person Perception', in Lindsey Aronson (ed.), *Handbook of Social Psychology*, vol. 3, 2nd edn (Reading, Massachusetts: Addison-Wesley)

Taguiri, R., and Petrullo, L. (eds) (1962), *Person Perception and Interpersonal Behaviour* (Stanford, California: Stanford University Press)

Thelwell, M. (1981), *The Harder They Come* (London: Pluto Press)

Vernon, P. (1963), *Personality Assessment: A Critical Survey* (London: Methuen)

Voorhoeve, J. (1971), 'Church Creole and Pagan Cults', in D. Hymes (ed.), *Pidginization and Creolization of Languages* (Cambridge: Cambridge University Press)

Voorhoeve, J. (1975), *Creole Drum* (New Haven, Connecticut: Yale University Press)

Walcott, D. (1982), *The Fortunate Traveller* (London: Faber & Faber)

Walvin, J. (1971), *The Black Presence* (London: Orbach & Chambers)

Walvin, J. (1973), *The Negro and English Society 1555–1945* (London: Allen Lane)

Williams, E. (1964), *Capitalism and Slavery* (London: André Deutsch)

Williams, F. (1984), *see News for Babylon*

Wilson, T. (1984), *see News for Babylon*

Further Reading

Below is a select reading list of books on black language and culture from both sides of the Atlantic. Emphasis has been placed on the Afro-Caribbean/British connection but a number of particularly relevant and readable works on black America and on Africa are cited. Throughout literary works are marked with an asterisk (*)

Teachers in search of materials and lists of speakers on topics relevant to this book should contact Afro-Caribbean Education Resources (ACER) Project, Wyvil Road School, Wyvil Road, London SW8 2TJ. A computerized databank on ephemeral (non-ISBN) teaching materials, Access to Information on Multicultural Education Resources (AIMER), is based at Bulmershe College of Higher Education, Reading RG6 1HY.

Group 1: Black Language and Culture in Britain

*ACER (1982), *Elaine Clair's Collected Essays and Poems* (London: ACER)

*Agard, J. (1985), *Mangoes and Bullets* (London: Pluto Press)

Allen, S. (1982), 'Confusing Categories and Neglecting Contradictions', in E. Cashmore and B. Troyna (eds), *Black Youth in Crisis* (London: George Allen & Unwin). A useful criticism of standard sociology on blacks

*Berry, J. (ed.) (1976), *Bluefoot Traveller: An Anthology of West Indian Poets in Britain* (London: Limestone Publications)

*Berry, J. (1979), *Fractured Circles* (London: New Beacon Books)

*Berry, J. (ed.) (1984), *News for Babylon: The Chatto Book of West-indian-British Poetry* (London: Chatto & Windus). See also all the titles mentioned in James Berry's chapter, 'The Literature of the Black Experience'

*Berry, J. (1985), *Chain of Days* (London: Oxford University Press)

*Bloom, V. (1983), *Touch mi. Tell mi!* (London: Bogle L'Ouverture)

Breinburg, P. (1974), 'Language and Education Failure – Cockney and Creole', Ph.D. thesis, University of Keele

*Breinburg, P. (1976 onwards), *Sally-Ann* series (Oxford: Bodley Head). Books with positive black images. *See also the Sean* series

Bryan, B., et al. (1985), *Heart of the Race: Black Women's Lives in Britain* (London: Virago)

*Campbell, L., et al. (1983), *Livingroom* (London: Black Ink). Nine short stories with an introduction by John Agard

Caribbean Communications Project (1980), a series of occasional papers on Caribbean language and dialect: No. 1 'English Creoles', No. 2 'French Creoles' (London: Arawadi)

Catholic Commission for Racial Justice (1982), *Rastafarians in Jamaica and Britain Notes and Reports*, No. 10 (London)

Centre for Contemporary Cultural Studies (1982), *The Empire Strikes Back* (Birmingham: University of Birmingham/London: Hutchinson)

Coard, B. (1971), *How the West Indian Child is Made Educationally Subnormal in the British School System* (London: New Beacon Books)

Commission for Racial Equality (1976), *Enquiry on the West Indian Community. Evidence on Education from the C.R.C. to the Select Committee on Race Relations and Immigration* (London)

*Dodgson, E., Smith, M. (1982), 'Motherland', *Ambit*, 91

Edwards, V. K. (1976), 'West Indian Language and Comprehension', unpublished Ph.D. thesis, University of Reading

Edwards, V. K. (1979), *West Indian Language, Attitudes and the School* (London: National Association for Multicultural Education)

Edwards, V. K. (1979), *The West Indian Language Issue in British Schools* (London: Routledge & Kegan Paul)

Edwards, V. K. (1981), 'Black British English: A Bibliographical Essay on the Language of Children of West Indian Origin', Sage Race Relations, Abstract 5

Edwards, V. K. (1986), *Language Selection in a British Black Community* (Avon: Multilingual Matters). Jamaican Creole and English in Dudley

*Equiano, A. (1967), *Equiano's Travels* (London: Heinemann). First published in 1789, written by an Ibo who lived in England and the Caribbean

*French, L. (1983), *Her Story So Far* (London: Black Ink)

Fuller, M. (1982), 'Young, Female and Black', in E. Cashmore and B. Troyna (eds), *Black Youth in Crisis* (London: George Allen & Unwin)

*Garrison, L. (1985), *Beyond Babylon* (London: Black Star)

*Goffe, L. (1984), *Unfamiliar Harbours* (London: Black Ink)

*Goody, J. (1981), *West Indian Writing: A Selection for Secondary Schools* (London: English Centre). A bibliography

Heskovits, M. (1958), *The Myth of the Negro Past* (Boston: Beacon). A positive appraisal of the African/Afro-American link

*Ingham, J. (ed.) (1984–), Luzac story-tellers (series) (London: Luzac). A Caribbean series is planned, to be called 'Stories from the oral tradition'

*Johnson, J. (1978), 'Park Bench Blues' and 'Ballad for You' in *Race Today*, January/February, 'Ballad for You' also appears with glosses in Sutcliffe (1982)

*Johnson, L. K. (1975), *Dread Beat and Blood* (London: Bogle L'Ouverture)

*Johnson, L. K. (1980), *Inglan is a Bitch* (London: Race Today)

*Jones, D. (1984), *Black Thoughts, Young Thoughts: A Collection of Poems by Derek Jones* (London: Benji Publications)

*Lamming, G. (1960), *The Pleasures of Exile* (London: Michael Joseph)

*Lee, J. (1984), *Sometimes you Feel Like Ice* (London: Black Ink). Poetry by a ten-year-old boy

*Miller, L. (1984), *Pin-pointing 'Human' Realities?* (London: Inky Fingers)

*Richmond, J. (1979), 'Jennifer and 'Brixton Blues': Language Alive in School', in *Supplementary Reading for Block 5, PE 232, Language Development* (Milton Keynes: Open University Press)

Rose, E. (1969), *Colour and Citizenship* (London: Institute of Race Relations/Oxford: Oxford University Press)

Rosen, H., and Burgess, A. (1980), *Languages and Dialects of London School Children: An Investigation* (London: Ward Lock)

*Selvon, S. (1966), *Lonely Londoners* (London: MacGibbon). A novel with highly successful use of black language. See also the titles mentioned in James Berry's chapter, 'The Literature of the Black Experience'

*Smith, M. (1982), *Bad Friday* (London: New Beacon Books). A novel

Stone, M. (1981), *Education and the Black Child: The Myth of Multi-Cultural Education* (London: Fontana)

*Sulter, M. (1985), *As a Black Woman* (London: Akira). The experience of a Scottish black woman. See also Williams (1985) and other titles in the Akira Press poetry series

Sutcliffe, D. (1976), 'Hou dem taak in Bedford sa!', *Multiracial School*, Autumn issue

Sutcliffe, D. (1978), 'The Language of First and Second Generation West Indian Children in Bedfordshire', unpublished M.Ed. thesis, University of Leicester

Sutcliffe, D. (1982), *British Black English* (Oxford: Basil Blackwell)

Sutcliffe, D. (forthcoming), *Code-Switching and Language Symbolism: Language and a British Black Community* (Avon: Multilingual Matters)

Talking Blues (1976) (London: Centerprise). Poems from the youth

Taylor, M. J. (1981), *Caught Between: A Review of Research into the Education of Pupils of West Indian Origin* (Windsor: NFER-Nelson). A useful review of largely uninspired research

Thomas, R. (1978), 'Infringement and Vindication', M.A. (Ed.) thesis, Institute of Education, London

Tomlin, C. (1981), 'The Extent to which West Indian Linguistic Differences Hinder or Enhance Learning', dissertation, Dudley College of Education

Walvin, J. (1973), *Blacks and Whites* (Harmondsworth: Penguin Books)

*Williams, F. (1985), *Leggo de Pen* (London: Akira). Definitely to be recommended

*Wilson, T-Bone (1980), *Counterblast* (London: Karnak)

*Zephaniah, B. (1980), *Pen Rhythm* (London: Page One/East End Print Workshop Co-operative)

*Zephaniah, B. (1985), *The Dread Affair: Collected Poems* (London: Arrow Books)

Group 2: Language and Culture in the Caribbean and Africa

Abrahams, R. (1972), 'Training of the Man of Words in Talking Sweet', *Language in Society*, 1

*African Writers Series, twenty-five titles (London: Heinemann)

Alleyne, M. (1980), *Comparative Afro-American* (Ann Arbor, Michigan: Karoma Press)

Allsopp, R. (1972), *Some Suprasegmental Features of Caribbean English and Their Relevance in the Classroom* (Cave Hill: University of the West Indies)

Allsopp, R. (n.d.), *Africanism in the Idiom of Caribbean English*, Occasional Paper No. 6, Society for Caribbean Linguistics, St Augustine, Trinidad

*Appiah, P. (1967), *Tales of an Ashanti Father* (London: André Deutsch)

Ayisi, E. (1979), *An Introduction to the Study of African Culture* (London: Heinemann)

Bailey, B. L. (1966), *Jamaican Creole Syntax* (Cambridge: Cambridge University Press)

Bailey, B. L. (1971), 'Can Dialect Boundaries be Defined?', in D. Hymes (ed.), *Pidginization and Creolization of Languages* (Cambridge: Cambridge University Press)

Barrett, L. (1976), *The Sun and the Drum: African Roots in Jamaican Folk Tradition* (London: Heinemann)

Bebey, F. (1975), *African Music: A People's Art* (Westport, Virginia: Lawrence Hill)

Beckwith, M. (1929), *Black Roadways: A Study of Jamaican Folk Life* (Chapel Hill, North Carolina: University of North Carolina Press)

*Bennett, L. (1957), *Anancy Stories and Dialect Verse* (Kingston, Jamaica: Sangsters)

*Bennett, L. (1966), *Jamaican Labrish* (Kingston, Jamaica: Sangsters)

*Berry, J. (1980), *Beat Bush Fe Partridge* (London: Akira). Long poem composed of Caribbean proverbs

Bickerton, D. (1981), *Roots of Language* (Ann Arbor, Michigan: Karoma Press). The argument *against* African syntax in Creoles

*Black Ink (1980), *Black Eye Perceptions* (London: Black Ink)

*Braithwaite, E. (1967), *Rights of Passage* (London: Oxford University Press)

Carrington, L. D. (ed.) (1984), *Studies in Caribbean Language* (St Augustine: University of West Indies, School of Education)

Cassidy, F. (1961), *Jamaica Talk: Three Hundred Years of the English* (London: Macmillan, for the University of Jamaica)

Cassidy, F., and Le Page, R. (1980), *Dictionary of Jamaican English*, 2nd edn (Cambridge: Cambridge University Press)

Comhaire-Sylvain, S. (1936), *Le Créole haitien, morphologie et syntaxe* (Wetteren: De Meester; Port-au-Prince, Haiti, with the author). BM ref. 12911, dd19. Authoritative

Comhaire-Sylvain, S. (1937–8), 'Creole Tales from Haiti', *Journal of American Folklore*, 50 (1937), 207–95; 51 (1938), 219–346

*Cundall, F. (1972), *Jamaican Proverbs* (Shannon: Irish University Press). Reprint of 1927 edition

Dalby, D. (1970), *Black through White: Patterns of Communication* (Bloomington, Indiana: University of Indiana)

Dalby, D. (1971), 'Ashanti Survivals in the Language and Traditions of the Windward Maroons of Jamaica', *African Language Studies*, XII

Dalby, D. (1972), 'The African Element in Black English', in T. Kochman (ed.), *Rappin' and Stylin' Out: Communication in Urban Black America* (Urbana, Illinois: University of Illinois Press)

Dalphinis, M. (1976), 'Various Approaches to the Study of Creole Languages with Particular Reference to the Influence of West African Languages upon Those Creole Languages', paper presented to the Africa Society, Kings College, University of London, 1976. Published in the *Caribbean Communications Project*, Occasional Paper No. 2, 1982 (London: Arawadi)

Dalphinis, M. (1981), 'African Language Influences in Creole Lexically Based on Portuguese, English and French, with Special Reference to Casamance Kriul, Gambian Krio, and St Lucian Patois', unpublished Ph.D. thesis, School of Oriental and African Studies, University of London

Davis, S., and Simon, P. (1979), *Reggae Bloodlines: In Search of the Music and Culture of Jamaica* (London: Heinemann)

Day, R. (1980), 'Varieties of English Around the World – Issues in English Creoles', papers from the 1975 Hawaii Conference. Specialist

DeCamp, D., and Hancock, I. (eds) (1974), *Pidgins and Creoles: Current Trends and Prospects* (Washington DC: Georgetown University Press)

Edwards, J., Rosberg, M., and Prime Hoy, L. (1975), 'Conversation in a West Indian Taxi', *Language in Society*, 4 (3)

Edwards, V. (1986, *Language in a Black Community* (Avon: Multilingual Matters)

*Farki, N. (1981), *Countryman Karl Black* (London: Bogle L'Ouverture). A novel portraying the life of Jamaican working people

*Figueroa, J. (ed.) (1966), *Caribbean Voices*, Vol. I (London: Evans). Reprinted 1985

*Figueroa, J. (ed.) (1970), *Caribbean Voices*, Vol. II (London: Evans). Vols. I and II have been published in a combined edition (London: Evans, 1971/Washington, DC: Luce, 1973)

*Figueroa, J. (1976), *Ignoring Hurts* (Washington DC: Three Continents Press)

*Figueroa, J., et al. (eds) (1979), *Caribbean Writers* (Washington DC: Three Continents Press)

*Figueroa, J. (1982), *An Anthology of African and Caribbean Writing in English* (London: Heinemann)

*Finnegan, R. (1970), *Oral Literature in Africa* (London: Oxford University Press)

Gilbert, G. (ed.) (1984), *Pidgin and Creole Languages: Essays in Memory of John E. Reinecke* (Ann Arbor, Michigan: Karoma Press). Extensive, specialist

Gorer, G. (1935), *Africa Dances* (Harmondsworth: Penguin Books)

Hall, R. A. (1966), *Pidgin and Creole Languages* (Ithaca, New York: Cornell University Press)

Herskovits, M. (1958), *The Myth of the Negro Past* (Boston: Beacon)

Hymes, D. (1971), *The Pidginization and Creolization of Languages* (Cambridge: Cambridge University Press)

Jahn, J. (1961), *Muntu* (New York: Grove Press). On African culture

*Jekyl, W. (1966), 'Jamaican Song and Story', *The African Folklore Society*, 55. Reprinted from 1907 original

*Jones, E. D. (1978, etc.), *African Literature Today*, especially issue 9, 'Africa, America and the Caribbean' (London: Heinemann)

Kebede, A. (1982), *Roots of Black Music: The Vocal, Instrumental and Dance Heritage of Africa and Black America* (Englewood Cliffs, New Jersey: Prentice-Hall)

Kenyatta, J. (1979), *Facing Mount Kenya* (London: Heinemann). Anthropology; excellent

Lawton, D. (1980), 'Code-Shifting in Jamaican Creole', *English Worldwide* 1, 2

Le Page, R. B., and DeCamp, D. (1960), *Jamaican Creole: An Historical Introduction to Jamaican Creole* (London: Macmillan)

Le Page, R. B. (1972), 'Sample West Indian Texts', York Papers in Linguistics, University of York. Useful texts from Jamaica, St. Vincent, Grenada and elsewhere

Le Page, R. B., and Tabouret-Keller, A. (1985), *Acts of Identity* (Cambridge: Cambridge University Press)

Lipschutz, M., and Kent, Rasmussen R. (eds) (1978), *A Dictionary of African Historical Biography* (London: Heinemann)

Longdon, M. (1971), 'A Comparative Study of the Structure of Jamaican Creole and Two of the Base Languages, English and Twi', unpublished thesis, available through Multicultural Support Group, Haringey, London

Mazrui, A. (1980), *The African Condition* (London: Heinemann)

Mbiti, J. S. (1969), *African Religions and Philosophy* (London: Heinemann)

Metraux, A. (1958), *Le Vodou haitien* (Paris: Gallimard)

*Moter, H. (1983), *Reggae Discography* (London: Music Sales)

Mouvman Kweyol Sent Lisi, various publications, including *Development of Antillean Kweyol* and *Handbook for Writing Creole* (PO Box 1097, Castries, St Lucia, WI)

*O'Conner, E. (n.d.), *Jamaica Child* (London: ILEA English Centre)

Owens, J. (1976), *Dread: The Rastafarians of Jamaica* (Kingston, Jamaica: Sangsters)

*Pollard, V. (1976), 'The Dust – a Tribute to the Folk', *Journal of Creole Studies*, 1, 2

Pollard, V. (1978), 'Code-Switching in Jamaican Creole: Some Educational Implications', in *Caribbean Journal of Education*, 5, 1

*Ramchand, K., and Grey, C. (1972), *West Indian Poetry* (London: Longman Caribbean)

*Ramchand, K. (1983), *The West Indian Novel and its Background* (London: Heinemann)

Reisman, K. (1970), 'Cultural and Linguistic Ambiguity in a West Indian Village', in Whitten, N., and Szwed, J. (eds), *Afro-American Anthropology: Contemporary Perspectives* (New York: Free Press)

Rickford, J., and Rickford, A. (1976), 'Cut-eye and Suck-teeth: African Words and Gestures in New World Guise', *Journal of American Folklore*, July–September, 89

*Ross, J., et al. (1984), *Callaloo: A Grenada Anthology – Four Writers from Grenada* (London: Youngworld Books/Liberation)

Sebba, M., and Todd, L. (1984), *Papers from the York Creole Conference, September 1983, University of York*. Contains papers on the language of black communities in Britain, the Caribbean and Africa

Sealey, J., and Malm, K. (1982), *Music in the Caribbean* (London: Hodder and Stoughton)

Taylor, D. (1977), *Languages of the West Indies* (Baltimore, Maryland: University of Johns Hopkins Press)

*Thelwell, M. (1980), *The Harder They Come* (London: Pluto Press). A novel that engages successfully with the rural/urban roots culture of Jamaica

Thiong'o, N. (1983), *Barrel of a Pen: Resistance to Repression in Neo-Colonial Kenya* (London: New Beacon Books)

Thomas, J. J. (1969), *The Theory and Practice of Creole Grammar* (London: New Beacon Books). New edition of 1869 original, on the French Creole of Trinidad

Todd, L. (1974), *Pidgins and Creoles*, Language and Society Series (London: Routledge & Kegan Paul). For the lay reader

Valdman, A. (1978), *Le Créole: structure, status et origine* (Paris: Editions Klincksieck). Specialist

Valdman, A., and Highfield, A. (1980), *Theorical Orientations in Creole Studies* (New York: Academic Press). Specialist

*Voorhoeve, J. (1975), *Creole Drum* (New Haven, Connecticut: Yale University Press)

Welmers, W. (1971), *African Language Structures* (Berkeley: University of California Press). Readable, excellent

*Wynter, S. (1984), *The Hills of Hebron* (London: Longman)

Zahn, D. (1970), *The Religion Spirituality and Thought of Traditional Africa* (Chicago: University of Chicago Press)

Group 3: Black Language and Culture in the United States of America, or the Americas as a whole

Abrahams, R. (1976), *Talking Black* (New York: Newbury House)

Baker, H. (1980), *The Journey Back: Issues in Black Literature and Criticism* (Chicago: University of Chicago Press)

Baker, H. (1984), *Blues, Ideology and Afro-American Literature: A Vernacular Theory* (Chicago: University of Chicago Press)

Bergman, B. (1985), *Hot Sauces: Latin and Caribbean Pop* (New York: Quill)

*Baldwin, J. (1964), *The Fire Next Time* (New York: Bell)

Cooke, M. (1984), *Afro American Literature in the Twentieth Century* (New Haven, Connecticut: Yale University Press)

Dance, D. (1978), *Shuckin' and Jivin': Folklore from Contemporary Black Americans* (Bloomington, Indiana: Indiana University Press)

Dillard, J. L. (1972), *Black English* (New York: Random House)

*Dorson, R. (ed.) (1967), *American Negro Folktales* (New York: Fawcett)

*Ellison, R. (1982), *Invisible Man* (New York: Vintage). A seminally important black American novel

Folb, E. A. (1981), *Runnin' Down Some Lines: The Language and the Culture of Black Teenagers* (Cambridge, Massachusetts: Harvard University Press)

Gates, H. (ed.) (1984), *Black Literature and Literary Theory* (New York and London: Methuen). Academic, excellent

Harris, R. (1981), *Being Black: Selections from Soledad Brothers and Soul on Ice* (with questions and notes) (London: New Beacon Books)

*Hurston, Z. (1935, reprinted 1978), *Mules and Men: Negro Folktales and Voodoo Practices in the South* (Bloomington, Indiana: Indiana University Press)

*Hurston, Z. (1979), *I Love Myself When I'm Laughing* (Westbury, New York: The Feminist Press). Reader, edited by Alice Walker

*Jackson, B. (1967), *The Negro and his Folklore* (Austin, Texas: American Folklore Society)

Kochman, T. (1972), 'Black American Speech Events', in Cazden, C., John, V. P., and Hymes, D. (eds), *Functions of Language in the Classroom* (New York: Teachers College Press)

Kochman, T. (ed.) (1972), *Rappin' and Stylin' Out: Communication in Urban Black America* (Urbana, Illinois: University of Illinois Press)

Labov, W. (1972), *Language in the Inner City* (Oxford: Basil Blackwell)

Levine, L. (1977), *Black Culture and Black Consciousness: Afro-American Folk Thought from Slavery to Freedom* (New York: Oxford University Press)

Mazrui, A. (1974), *World Culture and the Black Experience* (Washington, DC: University of Washington Press)

Mitchel-Kerman, C. (1969), *Language Behavior in a Black Urban Community*, Working Paper No. 23 (Berkeley: Language Behavior Research Laboratory)

*Morrison, T. (1980), *Song of Solomon* (St Albans: Triad/Panther Books). Superb Afro-American novel. See also *Sula* and *The Bluest Eye* by the same author

Smith, B. (1977), *Toward a Black Feminist Criticism* (Trumansburg, New York: Out and Out Books/The Crossing Press)

Smitherman, G. (1981), *Talkin' and Testifyin': The Language of Black America* (New York: Houghton Mifflin). In the spirit!

Southern, E. (1971), *The Music of Black Americans* (New York: W. W. Norton)

Toop, D. (1984), *The Rap Attack: African Jive to New York Hip Hop* (Boston, Massachusetts: South End Press)

Turner, L. (1949), *Africanisms in the Gullah Dialect* (Chicago: University of Chicago Press). Authoritative

*Wagner, J. (1973), *Black Poets of the United States* (Urbana, Illinois: University of Illinois Press)

Whitten, N., and Szwed, J. (eds) (1970), *Afro-American Anthropology: Contemporary Perspectives* (New York: Free Press). A classic

Group 4: The Rastafarians

Barrett, L. (1968), *The Rastafarians: A Study in Messianic Cultism in Jamaica* (Puerto Rico: Institute of Caribbean Studies)

Barrett, L. (1977), *The Rastafarians: The Dreadlocks of Jamaica* (London: Heinemann)

Bones, J. (1983), 'Rastafari Literature and Authorship', *Westindian Digest*, December 1982/January 1983. See also Jah Bones's column 'Words of Wisdom' in the *Caribbean Times*

Bones, J. (1985), *One Love: Rastafari: History of Doctrine and Livity* (London: Voice of Rasta Publishing House, Roslyn Road, London N15)

Cashmore, E. (1979), *Rastaman: The Rastafarian Movement in England* (London: George Allen & Unwin)

Garrison, L. (1979), *Black Youth, Rastafarianism and the Identity Crisis in Britain* (London: Afro-Caribbean Education Resources)

Iyapo, A. (1985), *Man of the Living, Woman of the Life* (London: Akira)

Nettleford, R., et al. (1960), *The Rastafarian Movement in Kingston, Jamaica* (Kingston, Jamaica: Institute of Social and Economic Studies, University of the West Indies)

Owens, J. (1976), *Dread: The Rastafarians of Jamaica* (Kingston, Jamaica: Sangsters)

Rasta International (1984), *Rasta Livity: A Basic Information* (London: Ethiopian World Federation Research and Repatriation Committee)

Reckford, A. (1978), 'Rastafarian Music – an Introductory Study', *Jamaica Journal*, II, 1 and 2

Voice of Rasta. Rastafarian newspaper published monthly by The Ethiopian World Federation, Roslyn Road, London N15

Index